THE CHEAP BASTARD'S® GUIDE TO

San Francisco

HELP US KEEP THIS GUIDE UP TO DATE

We would love to hear from you concerning your experiences with this guide and how you feel it could be improved and kept up to date. Please send your comments and suggestions to:

editorial@globepequot.com

Thanks for your input, and happy travels!

...STARD'S® SERIES

THE CHEAP BASTARD'S® GUIDE TO

San Francisco

Secrets of Living the Good Life—For Less!

Second Edition

Lauren **Markham**

gpp®
travel

Guilford, Connecticut
An imprint of Globe Pequot Press

All the information in this guidebook is subject to change. We recommend that you call ahead to obtain current information before traveling.

To buy books in quantity for corporate use
or incentives, call **(800) 962–0973**
or e-mail **premiums@GlobePequot.com**.

First Edition written by Karen Solomon.

Cheap Bastard's is a registered trademark of Rob Grader.

Photos licensed by Shutterstock.com
Text design by Sheryl P. Kober

ISBN: 978-0-7627-7303-9

Printed in the United States of America
10 9 8 7 6 5 4 3 2 1

CONTENTS

ABOUT THE AUTHOR

Lauren Markham is a writer, educator and refugee advocate who is proud to call the Bay Area home.

INTRODUCTION

As a SF native I may be biased, but for my (limited) money the Bay Area is one of the world's best places to visit and to make a home. Having begrudgingly moved away at age 13 to the East Coast, I spent my high school and college years dreaming of San Francisco and all it had to offer—and all I was missing—almost nonstop. Just as the West looms large in our nation's consciousness—go west! strike gold! be free!—so did San Francisco occupy my mind for nearly a decade as the land of milk and honey until I returned to make it again my home.

At first I worried it might not live up to the warping of over a decade of memory and my high-stakes expectations. It did—and I'm still calling the Bay Area home.

But dang, is it expensive here! As the pioneers could have told us, milk and honey don't always come cheap. Returning in my early 20s, having to pay rent and navigate my way as both a local and a newcomer straight-up emptied my pockets. It didn't help that I first worked as a teacher and then with Americorps VISTA (earning a whopping $840 a month) or that I am currently both a writer and a refugee advocate in the field of education. Needless to say, I don't make big bucks. Lucky for me, penny pinching has always come easy—and has, in fact, always felt like the best way to live and to travel.

And I don't just say that because I don't make much money. I say it because I've found pinching pennies to be act of engagement and thoughtfulness. It requires us to pay attention a bit more, and not just to the down-ticking sum of our bank accounts or the savings that still line our pockets. More than that, watching our cash connects the resident and traveler alike to our surroundings, the pulse of the street, the time of day, the source of our food, the time of year (the weather sure as hell wont tip us off) and, dare I say it, it makes us pay attention to the other human beings in the city we inhabit.

By searching out the deals and free locales we are making conscious choices and engaging with our community assets instead of purchasing mere packaged experiences—and we're maybe even hitting up places outside our normal routines or comfort zones. If it weren't for my love of fresh farm veggies and junky treasures, I may never make it to Alemany, for example, and if it weren't for my penchant for vintage clothing you'd probably never catch me in Pacific Heights.

Sure, I love good food and pretty clothes, but I prefer knowing where my food's coming from, and I've always sought out new-to-me items with past lives. Even if I could afford them, why wear clothes that any shopper could own? I'd much prefer clothes by the pound to clothes by Urban Outfitters. Things with a past life have a story, and it's fun to imagine the former uses for the sweater I don in the fog or the curbside sofa I sit on as I write this.

Plus, the cheap and free are often the more environmentally conscious options, choosing to ride our bikes instead of taking a cab, reusing materials instead of contributing to the factory industry of junk and waste. Anyone who's been in SF for more than a couple days is aware that environmentalism is a cultural priority—and that it can also keep your pockets packed makes it all the more sweet.

So, go forth and make some cheap choices for clothes with past lives, household goods with previous uses, outdoor movies nuzzled up next to total strangers, happy hours in neighborhoods you've never been, vistas that require you to walk rather than ride, literary readings from unknown artists willing to share their voices, and museums and galleries that benefit the communities they're housed in. Cheap is good not just because it's cheap (though of course that's damn good), but also because it gives way to more unique and thoughtful lives. From my own experience as a kid and adult in the Bay Area, this is a place where this very much holds true.

Enjoy!

—Lauren Markham

SECTION 1:

Entertainment in San Francisco

FILM:
CHEAP SHOTS

*"Hollywood money isn't money.
It's congealed snow, melts in your hand,
and there you are."*

—DOROTHY PARKER

Cheap is good, and free is better, and never is this more true than in the pursuit of entertainment. Those Hollywood fat cats are on notice: We spendthrifts are mad as hell, and we're not going to pay $10 to watch over-rated Scientologists strut around on the silver screen anymore! Instead we are digging our hands deeper into our pockets, and digging deeper into the pockets of the Bay Area that believe in the pursuit of cinematic happiness for a lot less dough. Cultural institutes, churches, parks, bars—and sometimes, even movie theaters—are all on board for a tight-fisted traipse in the dark. Close your eyes, and what do you see? The movies for less than most suckers pay. Sit back and enjoy the show.

Artists' Television Access
992 Valencia
(415) 824-3890
www.atasite.org
Thurs through Sun

The Catch: Most screenings are $4 to $6.

From the heart of the Mission, this tiny, bedraggled space has packed a real punch since it first took root in the community in 1984. Today this madam is showing her age, but ATA is still an unrivaled SF institution for young filmmakers (and visual artists and sometimes even musicians) to showcase their wares in an intimate and welcoming setting that would never fly in the mainstream. You won't find the latest rom-com (and you know you're better off!), but do expect cutting-edge artistic vision, nonnarrative explorations of the human psyche, documentaries galore, and even the occasional under-appreciated mainstream gem you missed in the multiplex. Check the website for the film schedule.

Bernal Heights Outdoor Cinema
Various locations in Bernal Heights
www.bhoutdoorcine.org

This neighborhood film event features terrific shorts from local filmmak-ers, many of which showcase the city itself. These are often family affairs featuring film crawls and block parties; picnics, minus the booze, are wel-come. Outdoor screenings run on SF's "summer" schedule—August through October—but BHOC has teamed with Bernal Heights Branch Library to offer free quarterly indoor screenings and filmmaker Q&A on the first Tuesday of

Cheat the Chains

Numerous theaters in San Francisco and the Bay Area—including the Embarcadero Cinema, Opera Plaza, the Bridge, the Clay, and the Lumiere—are owned under the national Landmark Theaters umbrella. There's not much one can do to avoid the $10 ticket price (heck, even the "bargain" matinees and kids' seats are still 8 bucks!), but they do offer a poorly publicized bargaining tool. Multiple ticket cards can be purchased at the box office only. A book of 5 passes sells for $38 (about $7.25 per ticket), but all passes must be used within 6 months, and they cannot be used for shows on Fri and Sat after 6 p.m. Celluloid-loving cheapskates with money to spend will want to take advantage of a book of 25 passes for $175 ($7 per ticket), which never expire and can be used anytime. Better yet, sign up to learn about occasional free screenings at www.landmarktheatres.com/Mail Bag/FilmClubIndex_frameset.htm.

February, May, August, and November. Add your name to the mailing list to learn about next season's offerings.

CELLspace
2050 Bryant St.
(415) 648-7562
www.cellspace.org/events

Versatile and multimedia-centric, there is always something cinematic happening here in between the visual arts and performance, though it's more likely to be DVD than celluloid. The "media arts cluster" offers low-cost video editing space and other film-related classes and work space, thus attracting the DIY moviemaking crowd. Low-priced screening fees mean the savings are passed along to you, the barely-making-rent viewer. Check the eclectic calendar frequently for the next unpolished, undiscovered gem. Films are usually $5.

Cinema Drafthouse Movie Night
At the Independent
628 Divisadero St.

(415) 771-1421
www.theindependentsf.com
Most Mon, 8 p.m.

The Catch: Two-drink minimum required, so this event is 21 plus.

One of the best bare-bones music venues in San Fran is now showing free movie screenings most—but not all—Monday nights. The selections are random to say the very least, but who doesn't recognize the combination of a stiff drink and a solid flick as the best way to ward off those new-work-week blues?

Cinema Heaven Encore
At the Melt Cafe
700 Columbus Ave.
www.noirfilm.com/screenings.htm
Thurs, 8 p.m.

The Catch: All screenings are free, but a reservation to screenings@hotmail .com is required for admission.

From *Mildred Pierce* to *Double Indemnity*, these classic black-and-white flicks come to life—as much as possible over the roar of a popular Irish-style pub serving pretty good Indian food. Films with a San Francisco theme or location are given preference, but any dusty gem of wisecrackin' dicks and troubled dames will please the loyal crowd of those who love the genre. These 16-millimeter treasures may be hard to track down, so join the mailing list for times and locations.

CinemaLit at the Mechanics' Institute
57 Post St.
(415) 393-0100
www.milibrary.org
Fri, 6 p.m.

The Catch: Suggested donation of $10 for nonmembers, free for members. Tickets are available at the door, but reservations (to rsvp@milibrary.oeg)are requested as it does get crowded.

Don't let the name fool you, you won't find grease monkeys tooling about here. The lovely 80-seat meeting room of this historic private library makes an SF-style social event out of watching a film. The Mechanics' Institute encourages viewers to come to the cafe a half hour before showtime and to stay after the screening for a group discussion. The film, from the library's collection of more than 3,000 classic, foreign, and American films, is formally introduced by established film writers and reviewers. Expect themes like a salute to John Huston, a tip of the hat to German comedies of the past 50 years, or a tackling of sexual politics and identity. Popcorn and refreshments are available, but they are not a distraction from the "salon" feeling of these weekly events.

Conscientious Projector Film Series
Berkeley Fellowship of Unitarian Universalists
1924 Cedar St., Berkeley
(510) 841-4824
Thurs or Fri, 7 p.m.

The Catch: $7 suggested donation (but no one is turned away for lack of funds).

Why is our world so screwed up? And more important, what can we do about it? These are the questions pursued in this regular film series covering everything from environmental justice to immigrant rights, sponsored by the liberal church's Social Justice Committee. Come, get educated, and move on. Subscribe to the film schedule at bfuusjev-subscribe@lists.riseup.net.

The Dark Room
2263 Mission St.
(415) 401-7987
www.darkroomsf.com
Sun, 8 p.m.

Bad Movie Night makes visiting this tiny black box worth it for any cheapskate worth his or her weight in ridiculous fun. "This is not an intellectual salon," the organizers warn. That, my friends, is an understatement. The Dark Room's rowdy denizens make for a welcome liberation from the buttoned-up multiplex crowd. Sunday's Bad Movie Night is a vociferous film fest featuring series such as "Bruce Willis's Not-So-Masterpiece" and "Superhero Movies That Are Less Than Super." Promoters promise to take all of the guesswork out of your night and assure guests that "Yes, it will suck." At least there's free popcorn. Tickets are $5.

Dolores Park Movie Night
20th Street and Dolores
www.doloresparkmovie.org
Second Thurs of each month, Apr to Oct, dusk

Few things are more wholesome than a cool summer's night under the stars, a Hollywood hit with a local bent, a visit from the Tamale Lady, and your contented pooch at your feet. D-Park organizers always manage to select that movie you've been meaning to re-watch for the past decade or the one that keeps coming up in interesting conversation. For zero bucks, kick back in a lawn chair, bring an extra blanket, and take in favorites like *Back to the Future, Chinatown,* and *Adaptation*. Some band usually opens, too, so come early or else sit wa-a-ay in the back, depending on your mood. Organizers are true-blue Delores Park locals and are entitled to a vay-k every once in awhile. Check the website before going over to make sure the event is on.

Film Night in the Park
Various locations around the Bay Area
www.filmnight.org
Fri and Sat, 8 p.m., May through Sept

Get on the schedule for this tasteful (and tastefully no-cost) outdoor movie project, courtesy of the San Francisco Neighborhood Theater Foundation and A.P.P.L.E. FamilyWorks. Thirty-two films—and good films, too, considering it's all family-friendly cinema—screen in nine parks in seven cities, prime time, with all the burritos and coolers full of beverages that you can carry. The line-ups are usually surprisingly eclectic from Hitchcock thrillers to '80s staples, and the occasional cult classic. The 2010 lineup included *Avatar, Wall-E,* and *The Big Lebowski*. Don't forget an extra blanket; this is San Francisco in summer, after all.

Films and Videos at the Public Library
(415) 557-4400
www.sfpl.org/news/events.htm
Times and locations vary

The library is your friend when your wallet is down and out, because, hey, your tax dollars have already paid for the services. When it comes to film and video screenings for adults and kids, the library branches around the city truly offer a great opportunity to cash in. Kids age 5 and younger are

SF Film Festivals:
The Most Noteworthy Events &
How to See Them for Free

DocFest, www.sfindie.com. May. Curated by the same group that organizes the San Francisco IndieFest, this has a similar vibe but focuses on documentary cinema. To volunteer, e-mail info@sfindie.com.

MadCat Women's International Film Festival, www.madcatfilm festival.org. Sept and Oct. An unpretentious, experimental collection of film, video, and more from around the globe. To volunteer, go to www.madcatfilmfestival.org/festival_info_volunteer.html or e-mail info@madcatfilmfestival.org.

San Francisco Independent Film Festival, www.sfindie.com. Feb. A loose, low-key, Mission District–centric film gathering celebrating young and bold DIY film and video. To volunteer, e-mail info@sfindie.com.

San Francisco International Asian American Film Festival, (415) 863-0814, ext. 213; www.asianamericanfilmfestival.org. Mar. The largest annual exhibition of its kind, showing 130 films in San Francisco, Berkeley, and San Jose. To volunteer, visit www.asianamerican filmfestival.org/attending/volunteer.php.

San Francisco International Film Festival, (415) 561-5019; www .sffs.org. Two weeks every spring since 1957. This festival attracts 80,000 people to more than 200 films. To volunteer, log on to www .sffs.org/about/volunteer.html or e-mail volunteer@sffs.org.

San Francisco International LGBT Film Festival, www.frameline .org. June. Since 1977 this high-quality collection of queer films has delighted audiences of 70,000 or more. E-mail through the website to volunteer.

San Francisco Jewish Film Festival, www.sfjff.org. July and Aug. Amid a host of other year-round projects, this Bay Area–wide event has launched similar festivals across the nation. To volunteer, e-mail jewishfilm@sfjff.org.

entertained almost daily with a revolving schedule of cartoons and age-appropriate media. And in the evenings adults can glue their eyeballs on everything from classics of Hollywood's golden era, the city's history in cinematic format, or first-run (OK, second-run) releases. The price for all this free media? No popcorn is allowed in the auditorium.

Goethe-Institut San Francisco
530 Bush St., 2nd floor
(415) 263-8760
www.goethe.de/ins/us/saf/kue/flm/enindex.htm
Times and locations vary

German culture in cinematic form, from classic to modern—sometimes subtitled, sometimes not. Special World Cup screenings also take place here, and on-theme refreshments are served. Germanophiles should take advantage of film seminars, workshops, and trainings here as well. Tickets are $5, free for students and members of the GISF.

Humanist Hall
390 27th St., Oakland
(510) 393-5685
www.HumanistHall.net
Wed, 7:30 p.m.

The Catch: $5 donation sometimes required.

This progressive church has been dedicated to "communitarian ideals committed to action for social justice" since 1935, and part of spreading the good word about the military-industrial complex, the filth of abuses of power and wealth, and other left-wing ideology comes forth in a weekly film series. Expect to get angry while watching spirited, underground political rants at the only solar-powered movie house in the Bay Area. Don't miss potluck refreshments and social hour at 6:30 p.m. and discussions after the film. If you're looking for something a little lighter, Humanist Hall shows feature films in May, August, and December.

Italian Cultural Institute of San Francisco
814 Montgomery St.
(415) 788-7142
www.iicsanfrancisco.esteri.it

The Catch: Films are free for students and members, but $3 for the public. Check the website for schedule of upcoming films.

The regular Tuesday-night film series is free only with Istituto membership, but the public is entirely welcome to other, more random screenings that take place roughly twice a month. Unsurprisingly, the films are either classic Italian cinema (such as a recent tribute to Mastroianni) or from the more modern era. Expect Italian with English subtitles, English with Italian subtitles, or, on occasion, just the plain ol' tongue of the boot.

Julia Morgan Center for the Arts
2640 College Ave., Berkeley
(510) 845-8542
www.juliamorgan.org

The Catch: Each ticket carries a $5 suggested donation.

Mostly family focused, this active and beautiful theater sometimes offers its stage to the silver screen. Expect classics like *Citizen Kane* or kid-centric cinema like *Mulan* on a periodic schedule.

La Peña Cultural Center
3105 Shattuck Ave., Berkeley
(510) 849-2568
www.lapena.org

The Catch: Many events are free, but some include a suggested donation.

This Latin cultural center focuses on music and poetry events, but it also hosts film events like the small but proud International Latino Film Festival, the Arab Women Film Series, and the International Disability Film Festival. View the online calendar to find out what's happening now.

Mob-Mov
Various locations, Berkeley
www.mobmov.org

Short for "mobile movie," this cinematic happening for artistic tightwads is the bastard child of a drive-in movie theater and a flashmob. Visit the website and sign on to the mailing list for the Berkeley shows: It's the only way you'll find out what films are playing, when, and where. The day before a screening, you'll be directed toward some sketchy lot in Berkeley. Add free candy, soda, and chips (more often than not), tune in to a radio station for the soundtrack and voilà—instant drive-in. This is guerrilla theater at its best, enjoyed from the comfort of your own auto's bucket seats. Sustainable, do-it-yourself, and oh-so-Bay—what's not to love? Tickets are $5 and up.

Monday-Night Film Series
Zeitgeist Bar
199 Valencia St.
(415) 255-7505
No set schedule; call for times

Weather permitting, this classic biker bar hosts the occasional outdoor film festival of locally made cinema in its mammoth beer garden. It's a perfect midweek evening, and the crowds flow in as freely as the outstanding house-made Bloody Marys and pitchers of brew poured behind the bar. Drinks are cheap, and you will want one. The smell of the barbecue pit is too good to resist, and well-priced grilled meat kicks Sno-Caps' butt any day. Get there early to grab your spot at the vast and packed picnic tables.

Revolution Cafe
3248 22nd St.
(415) 642-0474
Showings on Mon

Every Monday is movie night, featuring fresh local filmmakers. This vibrant space features fantastic jazz most nights but offers itself to us cheap, poor, and oh-so-appreciative cinephiles once per week. Call to find out which movie is playing this week.

The Red Vic
1727 Haight St.
(415) 668-3994
www.redvicmoviehouse.com

The Catch: Tickets are $9 for adults, $6 for seniors and children; $7 for adults for 2 p.m. matinees and Tues night shows.

A worker-owned and volunteer-staffed collective, this neighborhood land-mark recently celebrated its 30th anniversary (though its original location is just a few blocks away). This is a full-time art house and second-run movie theater with organic snacks, nutritional yeast for the 'corn, and rows of comfy, padded bench-style seating for those who get there early enough to claim them. Cult and underground classics are a mainstay of the Red Vic repertoire, but it also serves as one of the best places to catch those Oscar noms you missed in their first release for a few bucks cheaper. And of course, the Red Vic calendar makes for classic SF fridge decoration. Buy a punch card for 4 admissions for $30 (equivalent to $7.50 a ticket). Card-holders can use up to 2 admissions per show. Membership cards also get you a $1 discount at SF Film Society, SF Community Land Trust, and Garden for the Environment.

Roxie Cinema and the Little Roxie
3117 16th St.
(415) 863-1087
www.roxie.com

The Catch: *Tickets are $9.75 for adults, $5 for seniors and children. Bargains include $6 matinees and $5 for all shows on Mon.*

Proclaiming to be the longest continually running theater in the city, this relic turned 100 in 2009 and is still home to some of the city's most popular film festivals. The beloved Rox chugs along, and it opened a tiny second screen just two doors down (though popcorn must be purchased at the main theater, and the second screen isn't much larger than your TV). The seats are really comfy at this noteworthy art house for underground and local cinema, and kudos to them for being a great supporter of independent film from far and wide. Buy a punch card for 6 admissions for $26 (about $4.25 per ticket)—cash only, and only at the theater window a half hour before showtime. Cardholders can use only 1 admission per person.

University of California at Berkeley Art Museum and Pacific Film Archive
2575 Bancroft Way, Berkeley
(510) 642-0808
www.bampfa.berkeley.edu
Ticket sales: daily 11 a.m. to 5 p.m.

The Catch: *Tickets are $9.50 for adults; $5.50 for members and UC Berke-ley students; $6.50 for UC Berkeley faculty and staff and for all other students, seniors, people with disabilities, and youth under age 17. Additional features are $4.*

The Cheap Bastard's Lottery
(That You May Actually Win)

Penny-pinchers aren't about to blow their cash wad on a long-shot lottery ticket, but winning tickets to movies, theater, museums, club nights, dinners out, and so on is a horse worth a bet. Of course there are no guarantees, but with the exchange of a bit of your contact info to the marketing department (and perhaps a tiny shred of your dignity), local media venues that give away freebies every week are bound to fork over something to you eventually.

Here are the local venues that give away a whole lot of stuff to a smallish audience, thus increasing the likelihood of free goods for the truly tight and persistent:

KUSF request line, (415) 751-KUSF. This radio station of the University of San Francisco is college radio at its best and entirely plugged in to the world of no cover charges for live, small-venue rock shows and the occasional movie pass for intrepid callers. Projecting just 3,000 watts, its daytime listeners are likely to get through and win entry to something interesting that night. Listeners can subscribe to the mailing list for upcoming free events: kusf_fyi-subscribe@yahoogroups.com.

San Francisco Bay Guardian, www.sfbg.com/promo/emaillist.html. Add your name to the mailing list to find out about free film screenings, music events, and bar happenings with free and low-cost drinks and prize giveaways.

SFStation.com, www.sfstation.com/giveaways. Sign in and win dinners at nice places, free guest listings for fancy club nights, movie passes, DVDs, theater tix, museum entrance, festival tickets, and more.

The Hollywood blockbuster need not apply here. Cerebral entertainment runs the gamut from ancient Japanese puppet animation of Kihachiro Kawamoto to a tribute to smoky French actress Isabelle Huppert, and students and the college-minded clamor for the half-price seats that you won't find at the megaplex. The house also features arty video screenings, such as festivals of women documentarians and amateur film festivals, with the films' artistic visionaries often available for discussions and Q&As in person. Buy your tickets in person and avoid the $1 per ticket online purchasing fee.

Yerba Buena Center for the Arts Screening Room
701 Mission St.
(415) 978-ARTS (2787)
www.ybca.org
Thurs through Sun, 7:30 p.m.

The Catch: General admission is $8; $6 for students, seniors, and teachers; $6 for YBCA members.

This eclectic cinematic space is a true bargain for museum members, and unlike most cheap seats, these are actually comfortable, sophisticated, and will give your mind a workout, instead of your tush and spine. Make yourself smarter in less than 2 hours with pleasures the likes of the Human Rights Watch International Film Festival and more esoteric arty celluloid, such as a trilogy of vintage erotica, a Swedish showdown of films in real time, and psychedelic light shows from the 1960s. Pick up a YBCA Film Card, get it punched for 6 visits and your next film is free. Be sure to take advantage of free same-day gallery admission with the purchase of a film ticket. And if you check in at YBCA on Foursquare.com you'll get $2 off of your film or video ticket.

READINGS:
FREE VERSE

*"Diligence is the basis of wealth,
and thrift the source of riches."*

—CHINESE PROVERB

Science fiction, memoir, poetry—everyone with a computer or a pen can call themselves a writer, and many of them, from authors of *New York Times* best sellers to brand-new cellar dwellers, are very good. Sure, the big names always come to town to peddle their new hardback, but any word wranglers who can string two words together can find themselves in front of a small crowd and a microphone sharing their creative muse. Readings and spoken-word events fill the steamy air of coffee shops, upscale bookshops, the early evenings of popular bars, and any ol' community space where aficionados of the written word gather to sip, listen, and participate. No one is looking to get rich from his art, thus this is one of the city's bumper crops of cheap and low-cost entertainment. Don your thinking cap and dive into the pages of one of San Francisco's greatest brainy resources.

16th & Mission BART Reading
16th Street at Mission Street
http://16thmission.com
Thurs, 9:30 p.m. to midnight

Talk about a vintage SF happening: This weekly reading and performance series has no boss and no rules—come as you are and perform as you like. Situated in the grimy courtyard above the 16th Street BART station, the crowd ranges from transplant hipster to local poets, commuters, passersby, and folks who call the BART station home.

826 Valencia Volunteer Reading Series
At Amnesia
853 Valencia St. (at 19th Street)
(415) 970-0012
www.amnesiathebar.com
Third Mon of the month, 7 p.m.

Launched by literary "it" couple Dave Eggers and Vendela Vida so that Bay Area youngsters could have a place to write and find their writers within, 826 Valencia has now become a national do-good chain of free after-school writing and tutoring centers staffed by energetic and generous volunteers. Surprise, surprise, 826's prominence in the literary scene attracts volunteers with a writerly inclination—and they showcase their work in this monthly reading series in the dimly lit Amnesia amidst free-flowing pints of (unfree) local beer.

Bay Area Open Mics
www.bayareaopenmics.com

Literary, musical, and genre-blending performance art is what San Francisco's best known for—and as we're writing this some hip new event or reading series is being dreamed up in a park or smoke-filled apartment somewhere. So folks like us can keep in the know, some proactive locals have put together the Bay Area Open Mic Calendar listing all the ongoing open mics in town. The Internet: Stay in the Know.

Brainwash Cafe and Laundromat
1122 Folsom St. at Langton
(415) 861-3663
www.brainwash.com
Mon, 7 to 10 p.m.

Fun-loving multitaskers should head to Brainwash on Monday to cram your dirty clothes in the wash, stuff your face with a heady salad and plate of buffalo wings, and devour the sounds of local spoken-word artists come to share their flow. Anyone's welcome to read, so bring your scribbles. Need even more? Come back on Tuesday for the acoustic music open-mic night.

Litquake
www.litquake.org
Weekend in Oct

Litquake: It's nothing short of a Bay Area literary lovefest. This star-studded literary event takes place each October and can't be missed, as the writerly way is infused into the city's every nook and cranny, from dingy bar to packed community center to scrumptious restaurant to bargain bookshop to the regular city streets. There's too much happening, and in too many venues, to ignore. Hundreds of best-selling and semifamous names in every book genre, from mystery to fiction to politics to food and even to children's books, meet with their audience for intimate readings, workshops, panel discussions, and more. Check the website to drool over this year's schedule and pack your October calendar with writerly bliss. Got some extra time? Try volunteering your time to the Litquake cause (and have a chance to meet some of the Bay Area's, and the nation's, literary elite).

Queer Open Mic Night

Modern Times Book Store
2919 24th St.
www.queeropenmic.com
Every fourth Fri, 7:30 p.m.

The Catch: *The Open Mic is funded by audience donations, so optional cash gifts will be solicited from the public.*

Launched in 2004 and the brainchild and labor of love of local poet Cindy M. Emch, SF's seminomadic Queer Open Mic Night has found homes in the Castro's Three Dollar Bill Cafe and the Mission's Modern Times Bookstore. Poetry slams through the walls, and literary musings crawl up from the floorboards. This stage welcomes the talents of established local wordsmiths and emerging talent alike. This San Francisco neoclassic Open Mic is not to be missed!

The RADAR Reading Series

www.radarproductions.org
Traveling series; multiple locations and times

Powerfully prolific host and deeply enmeshed author Michelle Tea gathers panoplies of talented writers, often queer, left-wing and/or underground, "with the occasional superstar" to dazzle the lyric fantastic at this regular happening. At locations as varied and dynamic as Intersection for the Arts, the SF Zen Center, the public library, and the Verdi Club, participants and topics might include a Sri Lankan queer activist, interviews about Israeli and Palestinian relations, and well-known well-loveds like Beth Lisick and Trinie Dalton. Energetic Q&As follow each reading. To join the mailing list, e-mail SFSunday@aol.com.

Sacred Grounds Cafe

2095 Hayes St.
(415) 387-3859
www.sacredgroundscafe.com
Wed, 7 p.m.

Lo and behold, some of SF's most talented writers read during this regular weekly poetry showcase. There is no admission cost, but decent souls will buy a cup of coffee to keep the venue hot.

Great Bookstores with
Regular Author Readings & Signings

If they're on tour, you'll find them here . . . .

Adobe Book Shop, 3166 16th St.; (415) 864-3936

The Book Passage, 1 Ferry Plaza, #46 (Market at Embarcadero); (415) 835-1020; www.bookpassage.com. Note that most events take place at the Corte Madera flagship store in Marin County, but that many readings happen at this store in the Ferry Building.

Books Inc., www.booksinc.net. This left-coast bookstore chain has a number of locations—including two in the airport—but a slew of events occur at these SF spots:
* **Books Inc. in the Castro,** 2275 Market St.; (415) 864-6777
* **Books Inc. in the Marina,** 2251 Chestnut St.; (415) 931-3633
* **Books Inc. in Laurel Village,** 3515 California St.; (415) 221-3666

Booksmith, 1644 Haight St.; (415) 863-8688; www.booksmith.com

City Lights Bookstore, 261 Columbus Ave. (at Broadway); (415) 362-8193; www.citylights.com

Modern Times Bookstore, 888 Valencia St.; (415) 282-9246; www.mtbs.com

Pegasus Bookstore, 2349 Shattuck St., Berkeley; (510) 649-1320. Note that most readings take place at the Shattuck location, but sometimes authors visit the store at 1855 Solano Ave. (also in Berkeley).

Smack Dab
Magnet
4122 18th St.
(415) 581-1600
www.magnetsf.org
Third Wed of the month, show at 8 p.m.; sign-up at 7:30 p.m.

This is a truly free and truly open mic night—meaning that anyone is welcome to walk in and read/perform the words, music, comedy, etc., to their heart's content for 5 whole minutes in the spotlight, though the Castro location and the popular gay writers who host the night tend to give most material a bit of a bend. Featured readers kick the reading caliber up a notch, and author Kirk Read and great event-list congregator Larry-Bob Roberts usher in the unexpected. As they proudly proclaim, Smack Dab "make[s] the Castro safe for performance again." It's not a bar, so all ages are welcome.

The Speakeasy Reading Series
A Night of Poetry at the Bazaar Cafe
5927 California St. (at 21st Avenue)
www.bazaarcafe.com/calendar
Thurs, 7 p.m.

With rotating weekly hosts, the Bazaar Cafe gathers together a handful of poetry-centric Bay Area spoken-word artists to share their work with a mellow, caffeine-sipping, appreciative crowd of the same. Yummy and well-priced bites for those who like to pair words with friends *and* food.

The Word Party
At Cafe Virachocha
998 Valencia St. (at 21st Street)
(415) 374-7048
www.thewordparty.com
Every third Tues, 8 to 10:30 p.m.

The Catch: Suggested donation $5.

Open mic poetry and jazz just meld into one another at this collaborative art venue and vintage shop. Hosted by Jennifer Barone and Ingrid Kerr, the welcoming Word Party is well organized, well attended, and, true to its name, would surely make any soulful beatnik consider cracking a smirk in delight. Also check out their special events in other locations, such as a poetry party under the dome at SF's City Hall.

Writers with Drinks
The Make-Out Room
3225 22nd St. (at Valencia)
www.writerswithdrinks.com
Second Sat of the month, 7:30 to 9:30 p.m.; doors open at 7 p.m.

The Catch: $5 to $10, sliding scale. Check calendar ahead of time, as the date sometimes shifts to a different Sat when special guests come to town.

What variety meat is to lunch, WWD is to the literary scene. This stage, graced by SF's sexiest trans and well-polished writer, Charlie Anders, is a hodgepodge test-tube baby of what happens when erotica meets free verse, collides with stand-up comedy, and rams into the rear of speculative fiction. Arrive early—the comfy tables always fill—and cruise this essential gathering for the literary set. Names on the roster have included famed locals like Andrew Sean Greer, Maxine Hong Kingston, and Vendela Vida, and extra-special guests like Annie Sprinkle and Armistead Maupin. All proceeds benefit local nonprofits.

Yerba Buena Gardens Festival
760 Howard St.
(415) 543-1718
www.ybgf.org
May through Oct

Multiple free, multicultural, and multifaceted literary events are on the calendar for this summer-long free festival. See Free Outdoor Concerts (page 44) for more information.

Youth Speaks
www.youthspeaks.org
Various times and locations

For 10 years, Youth Speaks has encouraged teens and kids to speak their mind, write their stories, and sing or shout them to the world. There's always something to be heard and learned at their energy-filled, poetry slam–style gatherings. Their credits include a packed calendar of events that take place in coffee shops, street festivals, and hip-hop print publications. Almost all performances are free.

THEATER:
CHEAP SEATS

"This was a way to thrive, and he was blest;
And thrift is blessing, if men steal it not."

—WILLIAM SHAKESPEARE

Though San Francisco's grand theatrical dames are no Great White Way, super-pricey showstoppers can still be a free, or nearly free, ticket for the intrepid Cheap Bastard willing to work a bit for the fruits of the stage. If you like your theater smaller and darker, myriad actors' hothouses are tucked into nooks and crannies that offer great, innovative, or, er, interesting staged theatrics on the cheap. Tune in to the right deals and it's easy to save a buck or two if your schedule is a little flexible.

JUST **PLAIN** FREE **THEATER**

Free Shakespeare in the Park
P.O. Box 460937, San Francisco CA 94146-0937
(415) 558-0888, (800) 978-PLAY
www.sfshakes.org

This theatrical tempest swarms into a midsummer afternoon's dream of culture, gratis. Bring your own blanket, picnic, and Olde English–to–English dictionary to fully appreciate the splendor of this highly acclaimed company's community freebies that are to be (or not to be) in various parks around the region.

San Francisco Free Civic Theater
(415) 831-6810
www.sffct.org

A division of San Francisco Recreation and Parks, this adult theater company produces three to four shows that run from September through May. All participants are volunteers, and performances don't cost a dime. Most shows play at the Randall Museum Theater or the Eureka Valley Recreation Center Auditorium. Get in touch to find out what's playing or to get involved.

San Francisco Mime Troupe
855 Treat Ave.
(415) 285-1717
www.sfmt.org

The Catch: Donations are requested, and a hat is passed at the end of every show.

Since 1959 this political, satirical, and musical institution has been sticking it to the policy makers of contemporary life with full-blown, Tony Award–winning performances, scores, sets, and costumes. Contrary to what the name would indicate, this is not a showcase of whiteface mimes; rather, the subject of their stage is a broken-mirror mimicry of the current state of political affairs. The new season always debuts July Fourth weekend at SF's Dolores Park to a crowd of thousands and then tours into early fall at parks and outdoor venues in the Bay Area and beyond.

Smaller, Inexpensive Art Houses

These venues or traveling troupes feature shows that usually cost around $20 or less. Check what they're offering this season.

Brava Theatre, 2781 24th St.; (415) 641-7657; www.brava.org

CounterPULSE, 1310 Mission St.; (415) 626-2060; www.counterpulse .org

Exit Theater, 156 Eddy St.; (415) 673-3847; www.theexit.org, www .sffringe.org. They also need lots of see-for-free volunteers for the Fringe Festival in September.

Intersection for the Arts, 446 Valencia St.; (415) 626-2787; www .theintersection.org

The Marsh, 1062 Valencia St.; (415) 826-5750, (800) 838-3006; www .themarsh.org. Note that they also have an East Bay location: the Marsh Berkeley, in the Gaia Arts Center, 2118 Allston Way, Berkeley. Volunteer ushering opportunities are available for some performances.

San Francisco Playhouse, 536 Sutter St.; (415) 677-9596; www .sfplayhouse.org. Previews are just $18.

Shelton Theater, 533 Sutter St.; (415) 433-1226; www.shelton theater.com

Theater Rhinoceros, 2926 16th St.; (415) 552-4100; www.therhino .org

San Francisco Theater Festival

Yerba Buena Gardens, Yerba Buena Center for the Arts, and Zeum
Between 3rd and Mission Streets and 4th and Howard Streets
(415) 543-1718
www.sftheaterfestival.org

One day a year during summer, this all-day three-ring circus of local theater strives to expose audiences to a taste of the entire theater community, and there just aren't enough hours to see it all. From Shakespeare to Beatles' songs, from improv to puppet shows to one-act plays, 10 stages quickly rotate the scaled-down performances of 70 different troupes, companies, and groups of practicing performers and shed the spotlight on the broader SF theater community. This is a great place to pick up discount coupons for theatrical performances throughout the year.

Woman's Will

(415) 682-4167
www.womanswill.org
Summer, usually July through Aug

The Catch: It's free, but donations are encouraged.

Ever heard of Shakespeare's sister? If she had started her own all-female Shakespeare company, it might look something like this—women run and operated, and defying the ancient tradition of men playing all of the best women's roles. The entire Bay Area is treated to this intensely flavored summer stock; check the schedule for this year's events.

USHERING OPPORTUNITIES

American Conservatory Theater (A.C.T.)

415 Geary St.
(415) 439-2349 (volunteer hotline)
www.act-sf.org

One of the city's most prestigious houses—and the only one to offer New York–style free show access in exchange for showing paying patrons to their seats. It's a beautiful and dramatically vertical theater (if you get stuck on the third balcony, you might as well wait and rent the DVD). For the low, low price of nothing, alert theater fans who give the hotline 10 to 12 days' notice can request to work showing folks to their seats (and yes, sometimes that means hoofing it up all of those stairs) in exchange for lingering on to see the show gratis.

Cal Performances
Events at Zellerbach Hall, Hearst Greek Theatre, Wheeler Auditorium, and Alfred Hertz Hall
(510) 643-6710
http://cpinfo.berkeley.edu/information/job/volunteer.php

The only thing better than seeing exquisite performances like *MacHomer*, *Waiting for Godot*, Gilberto Gil, and a panoply of dance, music, theater, and family events is to see them without disturbing the dust on your wallet. Those willing to sing for their supper (well, sort of) can try to score one of the coveted ushering gigs in exchange for seeing the show smack-dab in the center of the UC Berkeley campus. Volunteers usually show up 90 minutes before curtain in the requisite white button-down shirt, black bottoms, and black shoes. Just before the show begins, any remaining seats are yours, but you must be back on the clock during intermission.

Eureka Theatre
215 Jackson St.
(415) 255-8207
www.42ndstmoon.org

Home to theater company 42nd Street Moon in the Yerba Buena Center for the Arts, this little company that could specializes in classic musical revivals, equipped with fantastic costumes and memorable and efficient sets. It boasts a mighty Wurlitzer and all the fixin's of picture-show heaven. Volunteer ushering is informal: Call the number above and find out which upcoming dates have openings. Show up an hour before curtain, dressed in the requisite black and white. Help folks find their seat, maybe sell a concession or two, and you're in.

Herbst Theater
401 Van Ness Ave. (at McAllister Street)
http://sfwmpac.org/topnav/general_info.html

The Catch: No advanced arrangements for ushering are accepted; first come, first served.

As part of the San Francisco War Memorial and Performing Arts Center, this massive, bustling theater hosts a tremendous amount of theatrical and performing arts happenings, including live discussions with notable celebrities, dance, music, and, of course, grand theatrical stagings beneath its classic red-velvet curtain. Volunteers should arrive at the door to the left of the box office 90 minutes before showtime. Black business attire is required (including white dress shirt and black tie for men), as is a flashlight.

Post Street Theatre
450 Post St.
(415) 321-2909
www.poststreettheatre.com

With tickets running as high as $85 a pop, you'll be happier to part with your time than your dollars. Groups of up to four people are often able to work together—and then see the show—at this top-notch, often-overlooked, first-class showplace. Call the number above and leave your contact info and preferred dates.

THEATER DISCOUNTS

Berkeley Repertory Theater
2025 Addison, Berkeley
(510) 647-2949, (888) 427-8849
www.berkeleyrep.org

The Catch: Opportunities for half-price shows have certain restrictions.

The Rep offers a number of ways for students and the general public to save money on theater tickets. First, there's HotTix, a limited number of half-price show tickets (limit 2 per customer) that can be purchased directly from the box office, in person, Tuesday through Friday beginning at noon after opening night. Anyone under the age of 30 can purchase half-price advance tickets, online or in person, for any show excluding prime time—Friday and

Saturday night and Sunday matinees. Be prepared to show proof of age. Students and seniors over the age of 65 can also buy half-price tickets a half hour before any show, based on availability, cash only. Other discount programs apply to alumni members and groups of 15 or more.

Magic Theater
Fort Mason Center, Building D, 3rd floor
(415) 441-8822
www.magictheatre.org
Tues night in season

The Catch: *The theater is sometimes rented out to external productions, including most of the summer, in which case a discount does not apply.*

One day a week tickets are sold on a sliding scale, and fans of the cheap seats can see a show for as little as $5 (or as much as $5 million). Group discounts are available for most shows—10 to 15 percent off for 6 or more tickets purchased together. With just 162 seats, there's not a bad spot to see the stage.

New Conservatory Theatre
25 Van Ness Ave.
(415) 861-8972
www.nctcsf.org

The Catch: *Cash sales only, with a maximum of 2 tickets per person.*

Every production at New Conservatory has one night that's open to the cash-strapped theater fan. On these special sellout nights, attendees may pay

Rehearsal Spaces on the Cheap
Located behind the Red Door at 975 Howard St., but otherwise unmarked, **The Garage** provides local artists with access to affordable rehearsal space and a supportive avant-garde community. Artists can apply to several Artist in Residency programs that encourage artists to develop new works and provide space free of charge. Interested artists should visit www.975howard.org or contact artistic director Joe Landini at (415) 518-1517.

what they can afford directly at the box office at 6 p.m. Check the calendar to learn about upcoming cost-saving nights.

MAILING **LISTS** & **DISCOUNTS**

Goldstar Events Newsletter
www.goldstarevents.com

Their promise: For the price of a movie, registered users can view live entertainment, almost all of it half price, and some of it entirely free. Don't expect an 8 p.m. Saturday show, but if your schedule is willing to bend, you can easily pick the low-hanging theatrical fruit at a pauper's price. Customize the information you receive based on what kind of stage show you'd like to see. Goldstar will also send you special deals for musical events, spa services, and more. A small processing fee applies for each purchase.

Tix Bay Area
Powell Street, between Union and Post (Union Square)
www.theatrebayarea.org

Same-day half-price tickets go on sale here every day, except for Thanksgiving, Christmas, and New Year's, beginning at 11 a.m. The lines can be long in the morning, when ticket selection and seats are at their prime.

Tix Bay Area Online
http://tix.theatrebayarea.org

Oddly enough, and just to confuse you, this online Tix booth has a different selection of shows than its physical location in Union Square. Easy to use and easy to search, the online service's half-price tickets for same-day shows are available at your fingertips, Tues through Sat, 11 a.m. to 5 p.m.

MUSIC:
FREE BIRD!

*"Money's a horrid thing to follow,
but a charming thing to meet."*

—HENRY JAMES

Is there any sound sweeter than freedom ringing? Maybe it's the ringing in your ears that you got for cheap? This town is alive with the sounds of nearly any musical genre your brain can muster, from samba to hard rock, acoustic to electronica. The variety of venues to enjoy them in is equally as varied, covering grassy knoll, grungy club, distinguished performance house, and everything in between. Cool or chaotic, start having a foot-tapping or booty-shaking good time at the city's broad offerings of talent to amuse your ears.

BARS, **NIGHTCLUBS** & **CAFES** WITH **NO** COVER

Abbey Tavern
4100 Geary Blvd.
(415) 221-7767
www.abbeytavern-sf.com
Thurs through Sun, 9:30 p.m. to 2 a.m.

Club Abbey features a college-heavy, mixed, laid-back crowd doing what few will dare to try in a sports bar: dance! And how could they not? Besides regular performances of raucous live Irish tunes, Abbey Tavern features a new live DJ or band every Friday and Saturday. On weekends you'll find a well-inebriated bunch high on life and a really cheap selection of draft beers. The truly penny-pinching will appreciate that on Thursday night, pitchers of Bud are $5 and pints are just a buck. If your two left feet can't jive, there's always the regular assortment of amusements like pool, darts, pinball, and sports on TV. Don't miss the Beer of the Month special: a different beer featured each month at happy hour prices.

Amnesia
853 Valencia
(415) 970-0012
www.amnesiathebar.com
Mon through Wed, hours vary

You'll pay up to 10 bucks to witness premium DJs here on the weekends, but midweek bargains in entertainment are to be had for the intrepid looking for a good time. Monday night is the highly acclaimed bluegrass night, where attendees ease into the week the mountain way and have easy conversation over the acoustic sounds from the tiny stage. On Tuesday you and your friends are free to make fools of yourselves at Amnesia's weekly open mic. And Wednesday is the entirely underrated jazz night, where a revolving band of the incredibly talented strum and pluck out 1920s-style jazz, including regular performances by San Fran favorite, Gaucho—not to be missed!

Bazaar Cafe
5927 California St.
(415) 831-5620
www.bazaarcafe.com
Tues through Sun, 7 p.m.

The Catch: *Be sure to purchase one item from the cafe in order to enjoy the show; it's worth it!*

Cozy, unplugged, and ready to showcase local acts, this is a favorite haunt for the aspiring original musician trying to grow a fan base and gain some performance experience. Thursday nights are open mic, and potential performers need to call or drop by in person to secure their moment in the spotlight. If the crowd goes wild, you may be lucky enough to be invited back to perform another night. If acoustic guitar and young, plucky singer-songwriters are your cup of tea, then this is your spot. The music series is so popular that the cafe has released its own compilation CD of some of its favorite acts.

Brainwash Cafe and Laundromat
1122 Folsom St.
(415) 861-3663
www.brainwash.com
Sun through Wed, 7 p.m.; Fri and Sat, 8 p.m.

All musical genres and socializing needs become swirled and agitated at this long-standing SoMa space featuring a great, priced-right cafe; lots of elbow room; a full Laundromat for your dirty dungarees' pleasure; and free, all-ages live entertainment every night of the week. The quality and style varies—sometimes the show is that dingy unmatched sock that gets stuck in your sheets, other times it's a cool T-shirt score. It's free. The kitchen closes at 9 p.m., and last call for washers is 9:30 p.m. Food? Laundry? Tunes? God bless one-stop shopping!

The Bubble Lounge
714 Montgomery St.
(415) 434-4204
www.bubblelounge.com
Jazz on Tues, 8 p.m. to midnight; DJs Wed through Sat

The Catch: If you want any other niceties, such as a table, bottle service, or valet parking, be prepared to pay through the nose.

Despite the fact that this West Coast outpost of a champagne salon is quite posh, there is never a cover charge to come soak in the effervescent atmosphere, hip jazz on Tuesday, and live, hip, ambient DJs Wednesday through Saturday when you can expect a mix of old school hip-hop and Top 40. Friday night features DJs on both floors, and it's the only time that dancing, rather than conversation, takes center stage. Otherwise, join the ranks of the other bubbly, beautiful people as they revel in an outstanding sparkling wine menu and überchic decor.

Club Deluxe
1511 Haight St.
(415) 552-6949
www.sfclubedeluxe.com

One of the best jazz bars in San Francisco, Club Deluxe offers a refreshing change from the usual Haight Street scene. No covers for weeknight shows, not to mention truly tasty Neapolitan pizza and a creative cocktail list. This joint is cash only.

Dolores Park Cafe
501 Dolores St.
(415) 621-2936
www.doloresparkcafe.org
Fri, 7:30 to 10 p.m.

The Catch: A hat is passed at every show, and suggested donations for the artist are appreciated.

Mostly acoustic musicians strum to a packed, all-ages house at this popular, parkside venue with lots of seating, caffeine, and beer. Check the online calendar or, better yet, subscribe to the newsletter to find out who's playing this week.

Gold Dust Lounge
247 Powell St.
(415) 397-1695
Daily, 8:30 p.m.

Open for more years than anyone would care to calculate, this is one of those bars whose happy hour starts at 7 in the morning, if you catch the drift, and this will either frighten you or entice you to investigate further. Should you choose the latter, know that the house band, Johnny Z and the Camaros (a revolving foursome of the same 12-or-so guys) will be there every night into the wee, drunken hours—playing classic rock from the 1950s to 1970s at more decibels than your ears have had to handle in a good, long while.

Harry Denton's Starlight Room
450 Powell St.
(415) 395-8595
www.harrydenton.com
Live music and DJs Sun through Tues, 8:30 p.m.

Deep house and classic R&B smoothly lilt from the turntables Sunday and Monday at this regular DJ and performance bar and restaurant off of tourist-heavy Union Square. Tuesday night, however, enjoy Denton's 360-degree views of the bay for free with no cover and a live band—usually sultry soul or some other genre to fit the classy joint's plush red decorum. Reservations are highly recommended, though reservations are not as critical at midweek events.

The Hotel Utah Open Mic
500 4th St.
(415) 546-6300
www.thehotelutahsaloon.com
Mon music, 8:30 p.m; sign-up between 7 and 7:30 p.m.

Rich with a century's worth of colorful history, today this low-rent watering hole and beer hall brings in bike messengers and the grumbling, anticorporate set for loads of beer and better-than-average bar food served slowly at reasonable prices. One night a week the revolving wheel of musical talents spins toward a free night for attentive audiences of real music lovers, and those who perform get to do so based on the luck of the draw of the hat. The *Bay Guardian* readers' poll voted this the best open mic in the area, so unlike most open mics, not everyone performing here is a newbie, and cheapskates will likely hear some unusually good tunes for a song. The show has become so popular that the Hotel Utah has known to host the event at other bars around the city from time to time. Join the mailing list to find out who's up this week. Piano and PA available. Stay late—a featured artist performs after every open mic at 10 p.m.

Johnny Foley's Irish House

243 O'Farrell St.
(415) 954-0777
www.johnnyfoleys.com
Most nights, 9 p.m.

This Irish-themed public house has a full lunch and dinner menu, though one needn't buy food to take in the entertainment. It also features a beer list as long as the Dublin winter is cold, and the staff never hits you up for money just for the privilege of walking in the door. The welcoming space features live bands Monday through Saturday, mostly 1960s classic rock, cover bands strumming everything from Garth Brooks to AC/DC and with a few romantic ballads and bluegrass bits thrown in just for show. The dueling pianos performances have become a Foley's favorite Wednesday through Saturday in the cellar: Patrons request songs of all genres, and things get rowdy!

Pier 23 on the Embarcadero

(415) 362-5125
www.pier23cafe.com
Mon through Fri, 8 to 11 p.m.

The Catch: Weeknight shows are always free, but most weekend performances will cost you between $7 and $10.

Classic jazz, salsa, reggae, honky-tonk . . . all genres take turns on this free stage popular with Bay-viewing tourists. A menu of seafood specialties, sandwiches, and pub grub rounds out the white-tablecloth experience. The daring can enjoy free salsa dance lessons on Wednesday night.

Revolution Cafe

3248 22nd St.
(415) 642-0474
www.myspace.com/revcafe2006
Most nights, 8:45 to 11:30 p.m.

Like the great revolution, the music may happen, and it may not. But when it does, you will be a part of it, and it will move you. This intimate, rickety, super-laid-back conversation joint features tons of outdoor exposure, good coffee, and great sangria. If the Mission is the epicenter of San Francisco people watching, then Revolution Cafe is your park bench. While you peep, treat your ears to everything from jazz and tango to sizzling ukulele, string trios, and an eclectic mix of all that can cram into this tiny space.

The Riptide

3639 Taraval St.
(415) 681-8433
www.riptidesf.com

Calling itself SF's "best little honky-tonk," the Riptide captures the laid-back cool of the Ocean Beach side of town. Every night features free live bluegrass, blues, jazz, and country, or the occasional Wednesday night surfing movie. There's a fireplace for those colder evenings and an excellent jukebox for when the live shows end.

The Sacred Grounds Cafe Open Mic

2095 Hayes St.
(415) 387-3859
Wed, 7 to 10 p.m.

Acoustic street musicians gather at this popular Haight-Asbury cafe for the opportunity to attend a musical forum where some come to play and some come to listen. Performers get 10 minutes or two songs to strut their stuff. A typical cafe menu of cheap eats, coffee drinks, and the like assure some small contribution for nearly every budget.

The Skylark
3089 16th St.
(415) 621-9294
www.skylarkbar.com

In the beloved armpit of the Mission, this tiny, dim watering hole has a cozy charm and appeal and live DJs kickin' it 7 nights a week (though you may be hard-pressed finding room to shake even a single body part). Monday features roots, dub, and reggae; Home Turf Tuesday draws a crowd with hip-hop and '90s classics; and Mixtape Wednesday is pure San Francisco energy. No catch here; there's never a cover.

Swig
561 Geary St.
(415) 931-7292
www.swig-bar.com

The calendar is packed with free and fun things to do and free and fun people to do it with. This modern, superstylish hangout has a lot going for it, including spectacular sipping cocktails and a scotch menu that would make your grandfather from the Highlands proud to wear the kilt. The entertainment, and the host of cushy vantage points from which to strike a pose and enjoy it, makes Swig a destination worth MUNI'ing for. Sunday night is an open blues jam, and Monday is salsa night. Tuesday through Saturday nights showcase some of SF's finest vinyl vigilantes, not to mention a plethora of indie, pop, '80s, Brazilian funk, dance hall, breaks, etc.

Thee Parkside
1600 17th St.
(415) 252-1330
www.theeparkside.com
Twang Sun, 4 p.m.

Country, western, bluegrass, rockabilly . . . "If it's got twang, it's our thang." This premier dive bar just gets better at weekend's end when the beer keeps flowing and the sounds can be enjoyed from the airy back patio. Unlike most free musical venues, this house of great sound is known for booking quality entertainment. As always, the Ping-Pong table is free. Daytime shows on Saturday are often free as well.

BARS, **NIGHTCLUBS** & **CAFES**
WITH **CHEAP** SHOWS

Blondie's Bar & No Grill
540 Valencia St.
(415) 864-2419
www.blondiesbar.com

Pints of martinis, people . . . Pints! Of! Martinis! If that is not an alcoholic cheapskate's best bulk buy, then you should just tuck a flask into your sock. Pair that with a hipster, high-energy Mission crowd of club kids and DJs spinning '80s music Friday and Saturday at Blondie's Wetspot (ew . . .), their ample dance floor, and you have a party. Or if you prefer it live, local talent graces the stage Tuesday through Thursday with funk, Latin, or jazz.

The Cellar
685 Sutter St.
(415) 441-5678
www.cellarsf.com
DJs Sun through Thurs

The Catch: Don't get too attached—by Thurs this is a Union Square bar with a dress code, bottle service, and VIP reservations. Enter on the weekend at your own risk.

Suckers shell out at much as $15 here on a weekend, but those in the know can party in style for nothing—if you time it right. Monday and Tuesday are the best nights to hit it, because not only do you get great house-spun dance hall and reggaeton, or old-school hip-hop, but there are $3 beers all night long and other specials on fancy cocktails.

Il Pirata
2007 16th St.
(415) 626-2626
DJs Sun and Wed, 10 p.m.-ish

This awesome, out-of-the-way Potrero bar is huge, the right amount of divey, and plush with big comfy booths, cheap beer, and decent parking. It's family owned and family operated, and you can tell! They host a revolving wheel of events, including salsa music the last Friday of the month, and bouts of live music of various stripes a couple of times a month. But they are best known for their mellow psychedelic trance DJs on Wednesday, and their late-night reggae on Sunday is guaranteed to make you late for work Monday morning. They also serve food; some options are noticeably better than others, but even the most hardened NYC transplant won't turn their nose up at Pirata's pizza.

Ireland's 32

3920 Geary Blvd.
(415) 386-6173
www.irelands32.com
Live music Thurs through Sun

Tuesday night is open mic night, and Wednesday night is karaoke for the hardcore Inner Richmond set, but otherwise there is a live band every night, and more often than not, it won't cost a penny to sit inside, Irish pint in hand. Genres vary and cover everything from traditional Gaelic to impressive Beatles cover bands to American rock 'n' roll. Throw Thursday night's beer-pong/flip-cup into the mix, and you've got a can't-beat combo.

Madrone Art Bar

500 Divisadero St.
(415) 241-0202
www.madroneartbar.com

Madrone has recently become the centerpiece of Divisadero nightlife, embodying the best of this spunky neighborhood. Music is the main event, but Madrone offers way more than bumpin' tunes every night; art installations, video, and design make a night spent here way better than your average sweaty-body danceathon. Thug jazz and funk rock from around the world heat up and spin out of control from the decks of these local music makers and shakers, and crowds line up around the block for big events like the Prince vs. Michael Experience. Sunday and weeknight events are often (but not always) cover-free. Even on crowded event nights, sneak in early—cover charges often don't start until 9 or 10 p.m.

Plough & Stars

116 Clement St.
(415) 751-1122
www.theploughandstars.com
Sun through Thurs, 9 p.m.

The Catch: Cover charge on Fri and Sat.

For traditional Irish music, this is the place—it was voted best Irish pub by *San Francisco Weekly*. But patrons are just as likely to find themselves clogging to bluegrass, gypsy jazz, and country acts. Check the calendar to see what's playing.

Rasselas Jazz Club

1534 Fillmore St.
(415) 346-8696
www.rasselasjazzclub.com
Live music Mon through Thurs, 8 p.m. to midnight; Sun, 6 p.m. to midnight

The Catch: There's a $7 cover for shows on Fri and Sat nights; otherwise the only cost is the price of a drink or two.

A 300-person concert hall; a second, intimate lounge; a fully-stocked Ethiopian restaurant and bar; and all flavors of jazz and related world beat sounds situated at the easily accessible intersection of Fillmore and Geary in the historic Fillmore Jazz district . . . what's not to love about this long-standing, family-run establishment? For the price of a drink or two to enjoy the show, audiences get a cozy, music-centric crowd jamming to Afro-Cuban jazz, melodic vocals, soul and funk, live dub, and more.

The Saloon

1232 Grant St.
(415) 989-7666
www.sfblue.net/saloon.html

Some say it's the oldest bar in San Francisco; some say it used to house the city's oldest brothel; some say it's the safest place in the city, having survived every major natural disaster in SF history despite its precarious North Beach location. Whatever they say, the Saloon is a San Francisco watering hole landmark, but you've just gotta go to really know. You won't be disappointed by the scene or the music, and the regulars here will show you how it's done. Blues and soul rule the dance floor and cheap, strong beverages keep everyone moving. No covers Sunday through Thursday; even the shows with a cover are a bargain as most lineups feature 2 separate shows.

Savanna Jazz
2937 Mission St.
(415) 285-3369
www.savannajazz.com
Tues through Sun, 8 or 8:30 p.m.

This mission-driven, community education–minded jazz venue stages live music 6 nights a week, with only 1 or 2 of those nights requiring a cash barrier to entry. The musically minded can also attend periodic lectures and learning series on the genre, provided gratis for those who just want to come and learn. More often than not, lounge lizards are jamming to the quality sounds of the house jazz trio, with a revolving guest repertoire, and the weekly, freestylin' jazz jam session. True aficionados come here for quality, real deal jazz; French, Caribbean, and West African eats; and a rightfully dark, black-turtlenecked ambience.

ALTERNATIVE **VENUES** FOR **FREE** MUSIC

Center for Contemporary Music (CCM) at Mills College
5000 MacArthur Blvd., Oakland
(510) 430-2191
www.mills.edu

During the academic year, September through April, this school of experimental performers, composers, performers, and unique collaborators holds several free community events that are always something to behold. From African ethnography to sound and fire to a soprano with a piano, there's always a great reason to cross the bay and boost your cultural IQ. Consult the online calendar to see what they're doing this season.

Community Music Center

544 Capp St.
(415) 647-6015
www.sfcmc.org

From classical to jazz to all genres of music worthy of study and refinement, this mission-driven hub of historical musical learning and preservation offers several evenings of mixed-bag entertainment a month, gratis. Audiences can choose from special engagement, faculty ensembles, and student recitals. Check the calendar to see what's on this month.

Chantey Sing at Hyde Street Pier

Hyde Street Pier
(415) 561-7171
www.nps.gov/safr/planyourvisit/events.htm
First Sat of every month, 8 p.m. to midnight

A 301-foot historic National Park Service bathing beauty, the *Balclutha* is the performance space where you are often the star. Spend an unforgettable evening aboard this classic ship singing sea chanteys as Captain Ahab intended—except that this is a fully sober songfest, where only coffee, tea, and hot chocolate are served in a mug that you bring yourself. This is an irregular event, but check the online schedule often, as it's worth the wait. Be sure to make a reservation before heading over.

Grace Cathedral

1100 California St.
(415) 749-6300
www.gracecathedral.org

No matter what your stance on God, Jesus, or religion, everyone loves beautiful buildings and fantastic acoustics. With your ears ready to receive this spirit, your soul will soar during this grand cathedral's periodic performances that are free and open to the public. Events could include anything from gospel choral ensembles to organ concerts on the church's magnificent instrument to an assembly of children's choruses. Check the calendar to see what holy sounds you can treat yourself to this month.

RobotSpeak Sessions

At RobotSpeak
589½ Haight St.
(415) 554-1977
www.robotspeak.com
Irregular Sun

Computer and electronic music come to robotic life at this regular boys-in-baggy-pants event in the Lower Haight's basement record shop. All are welcome to listen and observe as DJs spin their own flavor of turntableism and electronica every other month. Each 30- to 40-minute set features 3 performers and allows time for Q&A and technique sharing for other enthusiasts of the electronic San Francisco sound. BYOB, and it's a party. This event is unique and worthwhile, but these guys don't keep regular hours. Be sure to join the mailing list in order to mark these sessions on the old Google calendar.

San Francisco Cable Car Chorus

At Grace Evangelical Lutheran Church
33rd Avenue and Ulloa Street
www.sfcablecarchorus.org
Wed, 7:15 to 10:15 p.m.

The basement assembly hall is home to the public rehearsals of this acclaimed, long-standing men's barbershop chorus. All are welcome to sit and listen.

San Francisco Chamber Orchestra

(415) 692-3367
www.sfchamberorchestra.org

With performances all over the Bay Area, from Palo Alto to Berkeley to SF, and the vast majority of them free, this band of merry professional musicians is clearly motivated to spread the gospel of classical music to a culture-hungry crowd. If you're not sure if classical music is your cup of Chablis, this is a great way to find out. The regular family programs are a great way to introduce young ears to something beyond the scope of Raffi. Concerts are first rate and designed to educate but, by high-art standards, mellow enough not to intimidate. This is one of the area's most uncelebrated gems.

San Francisco Folk Music Club Friday Night Jams
885 Clayton St.
(415) 661-2217
www.sffmc.org
Every other Fri, 8 p.m.

The Catch: *Donations for snacks are solicited.*

The 1,000-members-strong organization devoted to acoustic and folk music from all over the world gathers at this regular event, but all are welcome, either to participate or just to listen. A singing room and 2 instrumental jam rooms run rampant and freestyle, from when everyone gets there until the last person leaves. Some snacks are provided. Can't get enough? Check out Hootenanny Night (equally free!) at Cafe International (508 Haight St.) every second Sat at 7 p.m. Still can't get enough? SFFMC puts on the Free Folk Festival every June at City College. Visit the website for details.

FREE **OUTDOOR** CONCERTS

Del Monte Square Courtyard
2801 Leavenworth St. (at Columbus Street)
(415) 771-3112
www.delmontesquare.com
Daily, 11 a.m. to 8:30 p.m.

From the heart of Touristville, in the axis of Fisherman's Wharf, comes a stage packed with multiple performances each day, featuring mainly music but also all varieties of performance art and comedy suitable for a family audience. This space has hosted the likes of Robin Williams, Shields and Yarnell, and Jefferson Airplane—though performances of this caliber are few and far between. If you're in the area, it's a great excuse to rest your feet and take in some tunes and a bay view.

The Golden Gate Park Band
Spreckels Temple of Music in the Music Concourse
Roughly 10th Avenue and JFK Drive, adjacent to the de Young Museum
(510) 530-0814

www.goldengateparkband.org
Sun, 1 p.m., Apr through Oct

In what is not only a local but also a national tradition—this concert series has been playing nonstop since 1882—this is 2 hours of wholesome entertainment at its best. Bring a picnic (but not the pooch!) and plan to spend the day amid stunning gardens of plants from around the globe, with musical accompaniment to match. The well-oiled band covers everything from ethnic explorations to Broadway, swing, opera, marches, classical, and more.

Hardly Strictly Bluegrass
Speedway Meadow
Fulton Street and 26th Avenue
www.strictlybluegrass.com
First weekend in Oct

After 10 years and counting, the only disappointing thing about this mammoth, music-filled festival is that it lasts only a single weekend. With dozens of performers spread over multiple stages, there's enough entertainment to last a week. Sponsored every year by a single dude—whom SF outdoor music enthusiasts consider to be the most generous man in the world—the weekend truly has something for everyone: There's top-notch bluegrass (strictly!) all right, and then there's everything else (hardly!), including truly well-known performers who dabble in bluegrass and beyond, such as Bonnie "Prince" Billy, Sharon Jones and the Dap Kings, Joan Baez, Billy Bragg, Gillian Welch, the Avett Brothers, and MC Hammer (yes, MC Hammer).

Bring a blanket, every snack in the pantry, and get there bright and early. Crowds are so dense it's a Herculean task to journey from one part of the park to another trying to see every thing that sounds good. We recommend picking a stage, setting up some turf, and sticking there if you can!

Jewels in the Square
Union Square
Geary Boulevard and Powell Street
(415) 477-2600
www.unionsquarepark.us
Wed 12:30 p.m. and 6 p.m., Sun 2 p.m., Apr through Oct

This new series began after the renovation of Union Square in 2005, presenting a stageful of live musical and miscellaneous entertainment ranging from barbershop quartets to country and from punk rock to religious worship services. Dance and theater performances mix up the schedule, so you're just as likely to hear salsa music as you are to listen to Shakespeare or watch fire dancing. A plethora of weekend entertainment abounds, but plenty of happenings are scheduled for the midweek lunchtime crowd.

Music on Mint Plaza
Jesse and Mint Streets at 5th Street
www.mintplazasf.org
Fri, noon to 1 p.m., July through Sept

For those of us slaving away all summer in downtown offices, Music on the Mint is the perfect lunchtime escape. *7x7* magazine rated it a "Best Meeting Spot," sprucing up those power lunches with Latin, jazz, swing, and mambo.

NextArts Concerts with a Cause
(415) 970-9005
www.nextarts.org

The Catch: *Shows won't cost you a dime, but they often request a donation of new and unused items for the homeless (such as new socks, underwear, or school supplies) in exchange for jazz, big band, and other performance band favorites.*

This small but growing nonprofit A/V equipment employment and job-training program has just begun to host outdoor summer concerts—including

---

Record Stores with Free In-Store Performances

Get on the following mailing lists to learn of free, on-site shows for underground and emerging artists.

Amoeba Music, 1855 Haight St.; (415) 831-1200. 2455 Telegraph Ave., Berkeley; (510) 549-1125; www.amoeba.com

Aquarius Records, 1055 Valencia St.; (415) 647-2272; www.aquarius records.org

Rasputin Music, 2401 Telegraph Ave., Berkeley; (800) 350-8700; www.rasputinmusic.com

RobotSpeak, 589½ Haight St.; (415) 554-1977; www.robotspeak .com

---

SF's first-ever nighttime concerts in public parks. These events are alcohol-and pet-free and include music, dance, theater, and comedy.

People in Plazas
Various locations in downtown San Francisco
(415) 350-7071
www.peopleinplazas.org
Mon through Fri, noon

These noontime events, sponsored by the Market Street Association, have existed for 30-plus years and feature more than 500 concerts annually to brighten up the workday lunch hour at plazas and parks all over Downtown, SoMa, and the Financial District. Genres can be anything from Latin jazz to blues, swing, or mariachi, featuring mostly local musicians. Consult the website for the full schedule of performances and specific locations.

Power to the Peaceful
Speedway Meadow in Golden Gate Park
Every Sept

The Catch: A $5 donation is requested.

This socially-conscious music fest is as much about fighting the good fight as it is about listening to live tunes. Michael Franti and Spearhead lead the event every year, joining their do-the-right-thing message with sunny, ener-getic music—the perfect combination to get SF in the groove. The event is big on environmental justice and human rights, and big names get behind the message every year, including Talib Kweli, Alanis Morrisette, Ziggy Mar-ley, and the String Cheese Incident. Don't miss the rather impressive a.m. yoga sesh before the performances are underway; stretch it out partner-style with hundreds of your neighbors before you get your dance on.

San Francisco Free Folk Festival
Presidio Middle School
450 3rd Ave. at Geary
(415) 321-0835
www.sffolkfest.org
One weekend in June, noon to 10 p.m.

During one summer weekend, just as they have for the past three decades, hundreds of volunteer organizers and performers come together to treat a flock of 2,000 to 3,000 enthusiastic appreciators to song, dance, percussion, and traditional folk sounds from world cultures and America's own backyard. Truly, there is something on the mile-long calendar to entertain every taste, including performances and workshops geared toward families, songwriters, choruses, and others. Check the website for dates and times.

SFJAZZ Summerfest
(415) 398-5655
www.sfjazz.org
June through Oct

Thursday evening in Union Square and Wednesday lunchtime at Levi's Plaza are two of the more popular outdoor venues for these nonprofit jazz masters, but the greater Bay Area is a stage during the season of more than 30 outdoor sound events. The caliber of the performers is excellent, and these short and often surprising performances are sublime.

The Stern Grove Music Festival
19th Avenue and Sloat Boulevard
(415) 252-6252
www.sterngrove.org
Sun, 2 p.m., June through Aug

Since 1938 the mammoth, underused outdoor expanse of Stern Grove has been home to 10 great music events each Sunday throughout the summer. Arrive very early, as this is one of the most popular outdoor concert series. Don't be discouraged if the lawn is full; hardcore Stern Grove goers plant themselves up and down the enchanted eucalyptus forest that surrounds the venue. You won't see much from there, but it's a one-of-a-kind way to listen to music. From rock and pop performers to the San Francisco Symphony, San Francisco Opera, San Francisco Ballet, and well-known Brazilian performers, there truly is a show for all tastes. It's a wonderful way to spend a Sunday afternoon.

Yerba Buena Gardens Festival
760 Howard St.
(415) 543-1718
www.ybgf.org
May through Oct

This monster free fest features 3 outdoor stages and hundreds of lively, talented, and (natch) free performances in the lush downtown gardens of this popular cultural center during the broad months of SF summer. Music, concerts, and events take place often, with an emphasis on a lunchtime music series of international sound. Dance, spoken word, literary events, youth and family events, and cultural happenings with a visual arts slant round out the extensive calendar. You'll certainly find something to suit your taste. Check the calendar to find out what's playing.

LOW-COST & **FREE** TICKETS **TO** LARGE **ARENA** SHOWS

Cal Performances
For events at Zellerbach Hall, Hearst Greek Theatre, Wheeler Auditorium, and Alfred Hertz Hall, see page 26 for more information on free shows in exchange for ushering.

Craigslist Tickets
http://sfbay.craigslist.org/tix

It's always the luck of the moment on this national buy/sell community bulletin board, but those fortunate few may actually be able to find tix to Madonna for a buck—though most tickets will cost a whole lot more.

Goldstar Events Newsletter
www.goldstarevents.com

Lots of concert tickets, many of which are half price.

Louise M. Davies Symphony Hall
201 Van Ness Ave.
(415) 503-5325
http://sfwmpac.org/topnav/general_info.html

First-time ushering candidates should call the telephone number above and leave their name and address; a packet containing information about

Free-to-Sing Karaoke Bars

Sip your drink slowly and you have a cheap night out watching friends make that Neil Diamond song happen. Tip your KJ a buck, and you'll be sure to sing like a bird.

Amnesia, 853 Valencia St.; (415) 970-0012; www.amnesiathebar .com; Tues.

Annie's Cocktail Lounge, 15 Boardman Place; (415) 703-0865; Tues and Sat.

Festa Wine and Cocktail Lounge, 1581 Webster St. (in Japantown's Kinokuniya Mall); (415) 567-5866. Every night of the week!

The Mint Karaoke Lounge, 1942 Market St.; (415) 626-4726; www .themint.net. Every night.

Silver Cloud Restaurant, 1994 Lombard St.; (415) 922-1977; Tues through Sun. Despite the name, you don't have to eat here.

Tango Tango, 1550 California St.; (415) 775-0442. Every night.

ushering and dress code will be mailed to you. After that, every Monday, this same voice-mail line is updated with dates when ushers are needed. Prospects will be instructed to either show up or sign up. There is free admission in exchange for ushering.

Nob Hill Masonic Center
1111 California St.
(415) 292-9150
www.masonicauditorium.com

Some ushering opportunities available, depending on the show. Call the in-house head usher at least a week before performances and inquire if volunteers are needed. Note that fall is an especially busy time ripe with opportunity.

War Memorial Opera House
301 Van Ness Ave.
http://sfwmpac.org/topnav/general_info.html

Those interested in being an usher here must write a letter including name, address, phone number, and a brief account of their interest in ushering and snail mail it to House Manager, War Memorial Opera House, 301 Van Ness Ave., San Francisco, CA 94102. No telephone or e-mail inquiries are accepted. Prospective ushers will be contacted if desired.

COMEDY:
CHEAP LAUGHS

*"Money is that dear thing which,
if you're not careful, you can squander your
whole life thinking of . . ."*

—MARY JO SALTER

Some say that the heyday of San Francisco's comedy scene has passed us by, and that the likes of Robin Williams, Phyllis Diller, and the original Purple Onion were the end of the line decades ago. But judging by the number of comedy events to crop up in recent years, and the reopening of some legendary venues, one thing can be said for certain: San Francisco is ready to yuck it up once again. We, the cash stingy, are not in the business of culture scouting or fortune-telling, and all we want is something to keep our wee brains entertained between beers. But we cannot help but wonder if we're in the midst of the next big wave, or if the joke's on us and we're just all wet. Either way, there's enough to explore right now to tickle our funny bone. Remember—free comedy is nothing to laugh at.

FREE **FUNNIES**

Alcove Theatre
414 Mason St.
(415) 431-4278
Fri, 10:30 p.m.

Looking for a late-night laugh? Head over to the Alcove Theatre for "Effing Free Fridays." Located just 1 block from Union Square, this event offers guests an hour and a half of free improv and cheap drinks every Friday, presented by EndGames Improv.

Brainwash Cafe and Laundromat
1122 Folsom St.
(415) 861-3663
Thurs, 8 p.m.

Local comedian Tony Sparks hosts this regular, longtime comedy night on a stage well worn with open mic. Full laundry facilities are on premises, and a well-priced cafe make it an affordable, and accessible, access point to the Land of Ha.

Cafe Royale
800 Post St.
(415) 441-4099
Every second Mon, 7 p.m.

Every second Monday, this swanky little jazz lounge hosts a free comedy night hosted by local comedian Cara Tramontano. Be sure to check out their extensive schedule of free events designed for a good time, including Beatles karaoke and screenings of cult-classic films.

Comedy Day
Sharon Meadows, Golden Gate Park
www.comedyday.com

Thirty comedians fill one stage for 5 hours of uninterrupted quality humor while you laze with your butt on the grass. Nifty idea, right? This could be why this event has been tremendously popular, drawing an audience of thousands for 25 years. Event organizers offer tourist hotel packages for those coming into town especially for the show. Check the online calendar for details about this year's event.

Harvey's
500 Castro St.
(415) 431-4278
Every Tues

The slant is gay humor, the cocktails are fruity and strong, and brave guys stand up among a boisterous, sometime inattentive crowd to strut their funny stuff, with results all over the map.

SFStandup.com
Can't get enough laughs? For the latest comedy happenings and deals, tune into the ultimate up-to-date resource for SF comedy happenings at www.sfstandup.com.

Kung Pao Kosher Comedy

New Asia Restaurant
772 Pacific Ave.
(415) 522-3737
www.koshercomedy.com

If you're ever stuck in town for the holidays, nothing says Merry Christmas like Kung Pao Kosher Comedy. A mammoth, all-star comedy showcase; a multicourse, lavish Chinese dinner; and a room full of Jews make up the Holy Trinity for this sellout annual event that always delivers delicious eats and well-seasoned, seriously funny professionals. The only thing better would be taking it all in without spending a dime, right? Well, if you have signed up for volunteer ushering, you arrive before the show, they feed you a great meal, and you get a free T-shirt. You show folks to their chairs for an hour or so and then you duck upstairs (in my opinion, the best seats in the house) to enjoy the performance. Make this your own holiday tradition, and it will be a good night for all, and for all a good night.

Sea Biscuit Cafe

3815 Noriega St.
(415) 661-3784
Sat, 8 p.m.

The Sunset needs a place to get funny, too, and this neighborhood cafe plays host to a wide array of practicing joke-telling folk tenacious enough to risk stand-up in front of a live, coffeehouse crowd.

CHEAP **TICKETS**

BATS Improv Theatre

Fort Mason Center, Building B, Suite 350
16 Marina Blvd.
(415) 474-6776
www.improv.org

The Catch: Many shows are as low as $5 if you purchase tickets online.

If you've got the lust for improv, and you don't mind buying your tickets ahead of time online, you can see this well-known theater outfit for as little as 5 bones (or max out at the door-price high of $20). For 20-plus years BATS has been making things up onstage at audience suggestion . . . and crowds just can't get enough. The cheap seats usually require a Thursday or Sunday performance, but if you can spread your weekend a little longer, close your eyes and make a wish, it will feel like a Saturday for sure.

The Dark Room
2263 Mission St.
(415) 401-7987
www.darkroomsf.com

This dark, dank, artist-run theater/performance space/bar/comedy club/ movie theater/whatever has one common thread in nearly all of its endeavors: They are pure camp, pure fun, and always something to laugh at. From sketch comedy to cabarets to small-time, locally produced exercises in public bravery that border on the blurry line of good taste and offbeat humor, this is the place to enjoy the show. Check the online schedule for events. Most shows are $10 or less.

Punch Line Comedy Club
444 Battery St.
(415) 397-7573
www.punchlinecomedyclub.com
Sun and Mon, 7 p.m.

The Catch: Tickets are $7.50 and under. All shows are for age 18 and over, and a 2-drink minimum always applies.

If the early bird catches the worm, then the worm that is latest on the weekends must catch the juiciest specimens. Or something. OK, that metaphor sucked, but these comic specimens are anything but for the birds. Sunday's SF Comedy Showcase tickets are just $7.50, and the Monday Comedy Sessions are a mere $6. Both events feature local talent good enough to play this national club. If you can't afford this, stay home and watch *Adult Swim*.

San Francisco Sketchfest
www.sfsketchfest.com

This fantastic annual event is definitely worth checking out, as it brings together a vortex of yuck makers that are certainly worth a splurge at full price (though most tickets, even at full sail, are still just around 20 bucks). However, our Cheap Bastard tip for you is as follows: Go to the website and join the mailing list. Midweek events with slightly sluggish sales are often sold 2 for 1 within a few hours or a few days before showtime. You can thank us later.

DANCE:
FREE MOVES

"There are shortcuts to happiness,
and dancing is one of them."

—VICKI BAUM

Some of us simply cannot wait to get into the studio and cut some rug, while those of us with two left hooves prefer to keep our relationship with dance one of appreciation, not participation. Either way, the expression and beauty of body movement and performance is a rich resource in this town, but with so many organized dance classes and events, one needn't be rich to enjoy it. Shake it, twist it, bend it, arabesque it . . . call it what you like. But from every ethnicity and culture, from formal to street, these spots will help you move to the groove of SF's dance scene.

DANCE PERFORMANCES

San Francisco Aloha Festival
Presidio Park of San Francisco
www.pica-org.org/AlohaFest/index.html

One weekend a year for the past 12 years, thousands of Bay Area residents have been mesmerized by hips swaying like palm trees at this celebration of Polynesian culture focusing on traditional dance and music. A boatload of island crafts, arts, and foods are also available from hundreds of vendors. Sponsored by the Pacific Islanders' Cultural Association, this is a pet-free, family-friendly (meaning no alcohol) event.

San Francisco Ballet
War Memorial Opera House
301 Van Ness Ave.
(415) 865-2000
www.sfballet.org

The Catch: Even with a discount, tickets are still $10 to $20.

If everything is beautiful at the ballet, then just imagine the stunning beauty and grace of supercheap, same-day tickets for the most prestigious dance performances in town. Seniors over the age of 68, students with valid ID, and members of the military can call the box office for discounted same-day show tickets, based on availability. These same demographics can also call ahead to book group-rate visits. Note that the discount is not available for the annual holiday Nutcracker extravaganza. Check the schedule for event dates and times.

Smuin Ballet
300 Brannan St.
(415) 495-2234
www.smuinballet.org

The Catch: Only some discounts available.

As one of SF's "other" ballet performance companies, tiny Smuin gets the edge by caring for the community and by making their flavor of ballet affordable to all. They offer all of the usual discounts—for seniors, students, groups of 10 or more—and hearty discounts to first-time season subscribers. But in addition, their season holds the promise of several pay-what-you-can nights, and they donate blocks of tickets to community groups who would otherwise not be able to offer their constituents access to the finer arts. This ballet doesn't just have legs. It also has heart.

Yerba Buena Gardens Festival
760 Howard St.
(415) 543-1718
www.ybgf.org
May through Oct

The Pulse on Dance

No one is ever turned away for lack of funds at any event at **Counter-PULSE** (1310 Mission St.; 415-626-2060; www.counterpulse.org), and this includes a wide palette of performances, such as dance, music, film, kids' happenings, mixed media, lectures, kooky art, local history, etc. CounterPULSE is mission driven to incubate grassroots projects and social expression of all stripes, and as long as they can afford to do so, they will bend over backward to serve this public need. They also offer gallery space, artist-in-residence opportunities, affordable space rental and office facilities, and more. No matter what a tightwad you are, spare what you can to ensure organizations like this one continue.

This summerlong massive festival of world culture features periodic dance performances. See page 48 for more information.

DANCE **CLASSES** & **PRACTICE** SESSIONS

ABADÁ-Capoeira San Francisco Brazilian Arts Center
3221 22nd St.
(415) 206-0650
www.abada.org

The Catch: *Discounts are for new students. No credit cards are accepted; cash and personal check only.*

Most classes in this butt-kicking Brazilian street art are about 12 bucks a pop, but new students on their first day can purchase a 4-class card for just $32—a great way to see if your body is up to the moves. Students age 19 and younger may be eligible for reduced rates and subsidized classes through a community grant.

Alonzo King's LINES Ballet (San Francisco Dance Center)
26 7th St.
(415) 863-3040
www.linesballet.org/dance/index.html

The Catch: *Discounts and free stuff are available with a $45 membership.*

Drop-in classes are usually $13 a pop, but if you're a serious prima ballerina you can buy your classes bulk rate. Plus, the $45 membership fee can stuff a lot of cash and goods in your tutu, including a free acupuncture consultation, discounts on massages and chiropractic services, discounts on dance-related tickets and merchandise, and, best of all, multiclass passes for as little as $9 each. Also note: The Dance Center opens its heart and its space to the greater dance community by allowing free use of the conference room (with a large table, 10 chairs, and monitor with VHS and DVD) by reservation; call extension 221.

Ballroom Dancing
Covenant Presbyterian Church
321 Taraval St.
(415) 664-5335
Mon and Wed, 7:30 to 9 p.m.

Your instructors, Bill and Dee Dee, are pure poetry in motion as they demonstrate the likes of the American-style cha-cha, waltz, tango, or, on occasion, the hustle. Learners of all ages bust a move to make Bill and Dee Dee proud. Beginners are welcome to drop by anytime. Admission is only $6.

Barefoot Boogie
8th Street Studios
2525 8th St., Berkeley
(415) 820-1452
http://sfbarefootboogie.com
Sun, 7:30 to 11 p.m.

There are a lot of "no's" associated with this event—no cameras, no food, no drinks (other than water), no scents, no smoking, no judgments, and, of course, no shoes. By casting all of these shackles to movement to the side, organizers hope to create a comfy, funky, eclectic space filled with world music from real DJs, true motion and body expression, and a rare opportunity for one to truly shake one's thing. The first-timer discounted fee is an $8 to $15 sliding scale.

Fat Chance Belly Dance
670 S. Van Ness Ave.
(415) 431-4322
www.fcbd.com

Nothing is sexier than those swaying hips of fury—particularly when those hips have a little meat on their bones. The teachers of this critically acclaimed, internationally performing troupe offer drop-in classes 3 days a week for every level of interest and ability, and it's a fat chance that you won't have a good time trying to look as good as they do. Proper attire is required, such as loose, low pants, skirts, or hip scarves. Zils (finger cymbals) are required—bring your own or buy them there. Admission is $10 and bulk-rate classes are available.

Harvey Milk Recreational Arts Building

50 Scott St.
(415) 554-9523
http://parks.sfgov.org

Part of SF Rec and Parks, this is hands down the best dance bargain in the city. A dozen or so classes are taught 6 days a week in all varieties—tap, country line dancing, capoeira, folk, and creative movement for children and adults—for nothing (or next to it). The schedule changes seasonally, so check the website or pick up a copy of the activities guide to find courses to suit your interest. Almost all are drop-in. While a few classes are housed in other rec centers throughout the city, this is the main hub of the dance department. Truly these courses bring the arts into the reach of those at every level of income—most classes are free, some cost up to $4.

Lindy in the Park

Golden Gate Park
JFK Drive between 8th and 10th Avenues
www.lindyinthepark.com
Sun, 11 a.m. (lesson at 12:30 p.m.)

Prolific and skilled Lindy dance teacher Hep Jen and her sidekick DJ Ken Watanabe take their dance lessons out of the club and into the open air for this completely fun, free, and informal weekly affair among the trees. The music plays until 3 p.m., with a short lesson in between to give park dwellers a few moves to swing by. The best part is that there's nothing to buy, there's no obligation to do anything further, and visitors are welcome week after week. Note that cars are not allowed in the park on Sunday, so ride your bike and enjoy the noises of the park and Hep Jen's stereo.

Hep Jen and Ken Watanabe have added a second dance freebie, Lindy in the Square. It's the same deal as Lindy in the Park, except it's held in Union Park from 6 to 8 p.m. on the first Wed of every month, May through Oct.

The Mandala Folk Dance Center

St. Paul's Presbyterian Church
1399 43rd Ave.
(415) 648-8489
www.themandala.org
Thurs, 7:30 p.m.

Have you been curious about folk dancing and seeking a venue to try it? This group, together since 1971, certainly bends toward the silver haired, but all are welcome. Know, however, that instruction only happens on Thursdays that are not the first or last of the month. Special events include on-site workshops and an occasional live band to keep things lively. Admission is generally $4, but Mandala also teaches a class on Sunday at Golden Gate Senior Center for those age 55 and over, where admission is just $1.

Mission Cultural Center for Latino Arts
2868 Mission St.
(415) 821-1155
Events hotline: (415) 643-5001
www.missionculturalcenter.org

While most public, drop-in dance classes are fairly affordable (in the range of $10 to $12), some highlights of the center's myriad dance classes are too good to pass up for the financially challenged. Many classes are offered for $8, such as Wednesday's Samba Jam for all ages. But do not overlook the many offerings of capoeira, fusion dance hip-hop, Tae Kwon Do, merengue, or rehearsal classes for the neighborhood's giant Carnival festival, all priced from about $2 to $4. Saturday has a good spread of classes for youths that feature dance but include some arts and crafts, each for just $2 to $4. And on Tuesday, Dance Azteca, a celebration in cultural movement for people of all ages, is absolutely free.

Pick School of Ballroom Dancing
380 18th Ave.
(415) 752-5658
www.pickdance.com
Beginners' classes: Mon, Tues, and Fri, 7 p.m.

This elegant little school of dance offers both private and group courses and recommends a program of both for new students. Those looking to scuff their heels on the cheap can take advantage of some of the finer points of the open schedule. Both the Sunday and Saturday open floor practices listed above may not provide the individual attention that many students of ballroom dance seek, but they do provide over 2 hours of dressed-up fun on the floor for a paltry sum. Beginners classes range from $14 to $16 per class, but beginners can also fill out a dance coupon on their first Monday, Tuesday, or Friday night class and receive a one-time class refund.

Queer Jitterbugs

At Queer Ballroom
Live Art Gallery
151 Potrero Ave.
(415) 305-8242
www.queerjitterbugs.com/volunteer.htm

If you're lesbian, gay, bisexual, or transgendered (LGBT) and you simply cannot get enough of swing dancing, no partner and no experience are necessary to let your feet join the club. Best of all, if you agree to help with some of the legwork, such as hanging flyers, working the door, etc., you will qualify for free entry to weekly and special events, including the annual gala ball.

Rhythm and Motion Dance

At ODC Dance Commons
351 Shotwell St.
(415) 863-6606
www.rhythmandmotion.com

Ballet, fusion, hip-hop, salsa, and yoga: If it means moving your joints this way and that, then this popular program newly housed at the fabulous ODC dance center boasts a packed schedule of classes for adults, kids, and teens and a competitively priced class with your name on it. Their philosophy is that no dancer should be left out, thus they offer a very flexible panoply of work-exchange programs ranging from one-time event volunteering to regular contributing positions, as well as access to some of ODC's most spectacular artistic explosions.

San Francisco Caper Cutters

St. Paul's Presbyterian Church
1399 43rd Ave.
(415) 751-3105
www.sfsquaredancing.org
Mon, 7:30 p.m.

Square dancing ain't just for squares, pardner, and this long-established group has been do-si-do'ing here on the quiet for years. Note that four couples must be present to make a square, but one can come stag and find a second half on premises. Most courses are for experienced dancers, but special beginners classes take place from time to time. Admission is only $5.

Keeping Dancers on Their Toes

When the clumsiness of the arts scene threatens to topple their best efforts, the local SF dance community falls into the arms of the **Dancers' Group** (3252A 19th St.; 415-920-9181; www.dancersgroup.org), a nonprofit supported by a number of grants that keeps dance artists in the air. This organization provides monies for aspiring visionaries to take risk in the arts, nonprofit umbrella status to help smaller dance organizations secure funding, and emergency financial support to help support the lives of dancers stricken with AIDS or other life-threatening illnesses. In addition, this service for dancers produces a number of annual publications, helps promote large-scale dance events, and supports the growth and longevity of the community as a whole.

San Francisco Feldenkrais Community Clinic
At the Women's Building
3543 18th St.
(415) 431-1180, ext. 11
Every Tues, 6 to 7 p.m.

Awareness Through Movement offers group classes in healthy movement for the general public, regardless of age or physical ability. A $5 to $10 donation is requested, but no one is turned away for lack of funds.

Shawl-Anderson Dance Company
2704 Alcatraz Ave., Berkeley
(510) 654-5921
www.shawl-anderson.org

The Catch: Passes are only good for 4 weeks after purchase. The discount deepens as you commit to longer periods—the best deal is the monthly unlimited, which can reduce the price for frequent fliers to as low as $6 per class

Most suckers will pay $14 per drop-in modern, jazz, and ballet class, but students able to shell out for a frequent-use pass can pay as little as $6 per class. Classes are offered for both adults and kids.

Studio Gracia

19 Heron St.
(415) 701-1300
www.studiogracia.com

If one doesn't mind trading time cleaning or manning the front desk at this spacious SoMa studio, then the full schedule of classes in salsa, Brazilian samba, or Argentinean tango won't twirl the cash out of your pocket. Inquire within.

Sundance Saloon

Space550
550 Barneveld Ave.
www.sundancesaloon.org
Thurs, 6:30 to 10:30 p.m.; Sun, 5 to 10:30 p.m.

The Catch: Admission for all night dancing and lessons is $5 for those over 21 (with valid ID).

Recently increased to twice weekly, this very popular LGBT event skews very heavily toward men only, but all are welcome. Two rooms feature $5 lessons in multiple styles of two-step, West Coast swing, and other finer points of country-western dance for a measly sum, with the real kitsch of country (just check out their website for proof). Dolly herself pipes off the DJ tables while boot-, hat-, and plaid-clad patrons two-step with pride. Dancing starts early and goes late, but lessons are given from 7 to 8 p.m. on Thurs and 5:30 to 7:15 p.m. on Sun. A full bar and coat check are available.

Zaccho Studio

1777 Yosemite Ave., Studio 330
(415) 822-6744
www.zaccho.org

The Catch: A $15 donation is suggested.

Serving where the city's need may be greatest, in the often overlooked and artistically ignored Bayview/Hunters Point District, Zaccho offers high-level, conceptual, mentally and physically challenging pay-what-you-can courses in movement and body performance for youth and adults.

SECTION 2:

Living in San Francisco

FOOD:
CHEAP EATS

"Never eat more than you can lift."

—MISS PIGGY

Few things taste better than the low-cost plate that someone else has prepared, and those who claim that there's no such thing as a free lunch simply weren't trying hard enough. When pots of our own homemade lentil soup begin to leave the taste buds dull, we hardworking, easygoing eaters can find myriad ways to fill our bellies on the sly. While by no means a complete list, here are a few favorite opportunities to chow down on the cheap—and don't forget that a Ziploc-lined messenger bag can hold the beginnings of the next meal as well.

HAPPY **HOURS**

Andalu
3198 16th St.
(415) 621-2211
www.andalusf.com
Tues, 5:30 to 10 p.m.

The Catch: *Tues only, and you will very likely get the hairy eyeball if you order nothing but the tacos.*

This is not a happy hour per se, as the list of 40 wines by the glass is still priced regularly, most around $8, though daily drink specials abound. But what makes this evening special in this bumpin', trendy, date-friendly environment, is the Tuesday Taco Night, when the dollar ahi tuna tartare tacos with chili, lime, and mango salsa are served fresh, plentifully, and all night long. If you were planning the beginnings of a night out on the town, this is a great way to save a few bucks on food to start things off.

Bar Crudo
655 Divisadero St.
(415) 409-0679
www.barcrudo.com
Tues through Sun, 5 to 6:30 p.m.

The recent arrival of this sleek, new raw bar offers yet another reason to head to the Divisadero Corridor for some of the best happy hour deals in the bay—when select oysters are only a buck a piece! Add to that two of the tastiest fish tacos in town for only $10, along with happy hour deals on clams, authentic chowder, and a variety of drink specials and you've got yourself one of NOPA's cheapest, most delectable destinations. Get there right on time; this hip little hot spot is comfortably packed by 5:30 p.m.

Butterfly
Pier 33 at Bay Street (the Embarcadero)
(415) 864-8999
www.butterflysf.com
Mon through Fri, 4 to 7 p.m.

Elegant white tablecloths, waterfront views, hordes of tourists, and an incredible daily menu of cheap nibbles and drinks cater to the palate of the secretively budget conscious. A mere 5 bucks buys the likes of duck confit spring rolls and ample plates of fried calamari, while beers are just $4 and daily wine selections a sweet $5 a glass. Or go nuts with your beverage budget and sample the Candied Ginger Collins, where gin meets ginger syrup and fresh lime, or the Cherry Blossom, where black cherry vodka mingles with lemon juice, sugar, and cranberry for $5. The bargain for what you see and get is one of the best on the bay.

Chaya Brasserie San Francisco
132 the Embarcadero
(415) 777-8688
www.thechaya.com
Mon through Fri, 4 p.m. to close; Sat and Sun, 5 p.m. to close

One of the hippest restaurants on the waterfront, Chaya Brasserie offers an all-night foodfest happy hour that, for the location and quality, should make you hop the bus to the Embarcadero, stat. Daily drink specials, including martinis, quality sake, specialty drinks (like the blood orange daiquiri) and wines (Sunday is half-priced bottle night) served fancy, hover at around $6, and numerous wickedly good and high-quality sushi rolls swing from $5.25 and up. Admittedly, it's not the cheapest way to find sushi in the city, but for the quality and location, this is a fraction of what most diners pay here during prime time. Chaya offers a more traditional bar menu of beef tenderloin, quesadillas, and the like to please even the fish-hating among us.

City Tavern
3200 Fillmore St.
(415) 567-0918
www.citytavernsf.com
Tues, 3 to 10 p.m.; Mon and Wed through Fri, 3 to 7 p.m.

The Catch: This well-known haunt for the hungry fills up rapidly, and no reservations are accepted. Prepare to get there early and get out quickly.

The Cow Hollow neighborhood simply buzzes with an eating and drinking frenzy when City Tavern offers its extensive menu of beers and food—good food, too, like turkey burgers, pizzas, chicken wings, and salads. They're practically paying you to drink and eat here, with menu items priced at just $2 each.

Hog Island Oyster Company
1 Ferry Building
(415) 391-7117
www.hogislandoysters.com
Mon and Thurs, 5 to 7 p.m.

Imagine this: It's after work and you're sitting outside the architecturally stunning Ferry Building with a view of Angel Island and Oakland across the water, watching the boats come in. That $4 pint of delicious, cold beer—Anchor Steam, Fat Tire, or whatever else is on tap—tastes cold and sweet and is the perfect foil for the outstandingly fresh and local oysters, briny, topped with a champagne vinegar mignonette or with just a dash of lemon and hot sauce. These chef's choice oysters are a buck a piece so they go down even easier. Safe to say you've landed in hog heaven.

The Lion Pub
2062 Divisadero St.
(415) 567-6565
Daily, 4:30 to 7 p.m.

These aren't exactly the most dependable bar snacks offered, but if you hit it here at the right time, the generosity makes it worth the gamble. In addition to an excellent spread of cheese, crackers, lunch meat, and crudités, sometimes sushi, smoked salmon, and chips and dips are offered as well. While you're awaiting the grub, take in the time-warp nature of the ambience—heavy wooden chairs, brass, dark decor, and fireplaces that come together to create the feel of a forgotten airport holding station. Note that there is no sign out front stating the name of the bar.

New Delhi Restaurant
160 Ellis St.
(415) 397-8470
www.newdelhirestaurant.com
Mon through Sat, 4 to 6 p.m., and 10 p.m. to midnight

Inside and outside of the dinner hour, this popular restaurant and drinking establishment lays it all out—samosas, pakoras, and tandoori chicken drumsticks, that is. The food is good, but positively ambrosia, considering it's a free serve-yourself appetizer bar. They make their money from the drinks you'll buy—$3 beers, house wine, and well drinks. No matter how you slice it, this is a bargain good enough to get on the regular rotation.

Ponzu
401 Taylor St.
(415) 775-9997
www.ponzurestaurant.com
Mon through Fri, 4:30 to 7 p.m.

The A-to-Zen Happy Hour is a great way to dissolve your workday at the bottom of a White Tiger (sake, Cointreau, lime juice, and salt) or a Tuk-Tuk (Gray Goose orange vodka, peach schnapps, cranberry, Thai basil, fresh lime). Best of all, several tasty dim sum bites, such as Kobe beef sliders and Chinese five-spice meatballs, are $3 a piece.

Restaurant Seven Fifty at the Hilton San Francisco
Financial District
750 Kearny St.
(415) 433-6600
www.sanfranciscohiltonhotel.com
Mon through Fri, 2 to 7 p.m.

They say Financial District, I say Chinatown, but we all agree that a bargain is a bargain. And while the drink specials change both daily and seasonally—plan on a fancy-schmancy hotel cocktail for about $6—the real cheap eats here are the food, where the menu of filling pub grub appetizers are half off and, coincidentally, the deal actually happens at a time when you

Ten Meals Under $10

Arizmendi Bakery, multiple locations; www.arizmendibakery.org. A network of cooperative bakeries that make organic, locally sourced, gluten-filled treats that warm the heart and fill the belly, Arizmendi also offer daily seasonal veggie pizza specials that make the snottiest gourmand drool. Pizza served from 11 a.m. to closing, $2.50 for a hefty, healthy slice; full pizza costs $18 and can happily feed three.

Good Luck Dim Sum, 736 Clement St.; (415) 386-3388. Nearly any dim sum joint along this stretch of Clement will fill the gullet, but this is one of the better choices. With three of these and four of those, two people can eat for well under $10.

Il Pollaio, 555 Columbus Ave.; (415) 362-7727. It's tough to eat in North Beach for less than a Jackson note, but these finger-lickin' chicken, soups, and awesome side-salad full meals are worth taking under your wing.

In-N-Out Burger, 333 Jefferson St.; (800) 786-1000; www.in-n-out .com. Normally fast food is fast food. But this is gourmet accelerated dining with a cult following and one of the few inexpensive and reliable eateries in the very touristy Fisherman's Wharf.

King of Falafel, 1801 Divisadero St.; (415) 931-5455. The sign says it all: BEST FALAFEL IN SF. That includes baklava, *shwarma*, and baba ghanoush to make your heart scream. And all for an unprincely sum!

would actually want to eat dinner. You can easily make a meal of the likes of jalapeño poppers, chicken nachos, garlic fries, mussels, and buffalo wings for about 5 bucks a generous plate.

Shima Sushi
601 Van Ness Ave.
(415) 292-9997
Mon through Sat, 5 to 6 p.m.

La Taqueria, 2889 Mission St.; (415) 285-7117. Every San Franciscan has a favorite taco and burrito joint, and sometimes that favorite can change by the day. But they all share one thing in common: heaps of food, dirt cheap, to fill you up for hours. This is one of the most authentic, freshest, and most popular—for good reason.

Lucca Ravioli Company, 1100 Valencia St.; (415) 647-5581. There's no place to sit down at this awesome Italian market, but a half sheet of the house-made Sicilian-style pizza for 5 bucks is a slice of cheapskate heaven and can easily feed three or four. Want to impress your friends with some homemade ravioli? Lucca's staff will roll you out a table of fresh dough for $5 for a half table (30 inches by 4.5 feet) if you get there on a weekday between 9 and 11 a.m.

Pakwan, 3182 16th St.; (415) 255-2440. Self-service Pakistani food that's robustly flavorful and cheap, with many curries around $5. Add naan for $1 and biryani rice for $2. Other SF locations: 653 Clay St. (415-834-9904); and 501 O'Farrell St. (415-776-0160).

Shanghai Dumpling King, 3319 Balboa St.; (415) 387-2088. Bring your appetite and a group of dumpling-loving friends, as this place is great for crowds. They offer a plethora of steamed and fried dumplings to fill both the carnivorous and vegan's stomachs alike—for cheap and faster than you can say "I'm full."

Tu Lan, 8 6th St.; (415) 626-0927. Don't let the Tenderloin location scare you off. This is excellent, freshly prepared Vietnamese food that's fast, cheap, and out of control.

Normally, cheap sushi is something to be avoided, but centrally situated Opera Plaza is home to this decent-enough sushi spot that really hits it home for a late-night post-movie bite. Large hot sakes and a menu of handrolls are just 3 bucks a pop during the magical hour of low-cost bliss. Take that, roll it, and eat it.

FOOD **STORES** & **FARMERS'** MARKETS

Alemany Farmers' Market
100 Alemany Blvd. (at I-280)
(415) 647-2043
Sat, 6 a.m. to 3 p.m.

About a million reasons exist to support your local farmers' market—the environmental benefits of local produce; the advance of a local economy; healthier, better-tasting food, etc. But we penny-pinchers know that there's more to it than a heartfelt mission—at farmers' markets, we can get our tomatoes and melons at a good price. The Bay Area is guilty of elevating the humble weekend produce market to Mount Olympus status, and the resulting $6 a pound for a bag o' apples is just too much dough. This is one of the few regular fruit and vegetable parades that boasts old farm-stand prices, great variety, and still supports the mission that makes waking up at the wee hours on a Saturday well worth the while.

Bargain Bank
599 Clement St.
(415) 221-4852
www.bargainbank.com

Though Bargain Bank used to sell all sorts of personal care items and sundries for the home, now the inventory is almost exclusively dry-packaged gourmet food from around the world, plus heaps of priced-to-move wine (seriously—like $3 a bottle) and other beverages. Ninety-nine cents can easily buy you a box of cereal, a bottle of marinade or salad dressing, some imported fancy cookies, and the like, making this a worthy stop when party planning. Their warehouse location (566 Minnesota St.; 415-552-7283) has a wine-tasting license, and you can try samples of most of the stock while you shop.

Bayview Hunters Point Farmers' Market
3rd and Galvez Streets
(415) 285-7584
Sat, 10 a.m. to 3 p.m.

This is another gem on the fresh and local produce circuit, where $10 can buy as much as you can comfortably eat in a week, most of which was grown by minority farmers to boot. It's a small market, but certainly worth a visit on a weekend during the season. Even luxury items, like blackberries and raspberries, are sold at some of the best prices anywhere in the city.

Grocery Outlet
2001 4th St., Berkeley
(510) 666-0670
www.groceryoutlets.com

This left-coast chain began in San Francisco in the 1940s, and its commitment to "bargain only" food and household items is still going strong. They buy bulk overstocked or bulk stocked goods and sell them at significant discount—everything from frozen egg rolls to Australian wine to hand soap and all that you can imagine in between, depending on the market at the moment. You never know what you're going to find, but there will be plenty of it, and it's sure to be cheap. A second area location is at 2900 Broadway, Oakland (510-465-5649).

L & M Produce Market
2169 Mission St.
(415) 864-1330

In truth, any produce market along Mission between 16th and 24th Streets is going to save you a bundle, but this is one of our favorites for reliability, freshness, selection, and a helpful staff. You'll find an excellent selection of the Latino grocery items that the neighborhood mandates (think fresh cactus, tamarind, dried chili peppers, and canned Mexican cooking sauces). They also have a great selection of Thai items, like fresh coconut, noodles, and curry pastes, for a fraction of the price of the big chains.

New May Wah Supermarket
707 Clement St.
(415) 221-9826

In addition to a dizzying array of superfresh fish, meat, fruits, and vegetables at rural China prices, this outstanding and mammoth Chinese grocery supercenter has all of the usual specimens that make shopping for food in another country interesting—pickled burdock, turtles on ice, and more

On Your Honor:
Delicious "Pay What You Will" Food Spots

A land where Eastern philosophy meets a spirit of philanthropy and boogies all night long with the trendy and the gourmand, it's no surprise that San Francisco's got its fair share of karmic "on your honor" eateries. These delicious offerings are just that—offerings, designed to feed those most in need. No one's gonna check your bank account or ask after your salary, but remember: There's no hiding from karma.

Karma Kitchen at Taste of the Himalayas, 1700 Shattuck Ave., Berkeley; (510) 849-4983. Staffed by volunteers, Taste of the Himalayas soulfully transforms into the Karma Kitchen every Sun from 11 a.m. to 3 p.m. When you get the bill, it reads "$0" and asks for you to pay it forward, however you can, so someone else can enjoy a meal in the future.

Cafe Gratitude, 2400 Harrison St.; (415) 830-3014; and 1730 Shattuck Ave., Berkeley; (510) 725-4418. "I'm grateful I have enough money to pay for this meal!" one might think (or say) at this raw, vegan, and astronomically expensive cult classic restaurant. Many of us may not be able to afford it, but Cafe Gratitude's Grateful Bowl is a sliding-scale, pay-what-you-will, grain-bowl menu option packed with nutrients that don't burn holes in your already fraying pockets.

San Francisco Food Not Bombs, www.sffnb.org. This local outpost of the national organization serves dinner to anyone who needs it every weeknight at the United Nations Plaza from 6:30 to 7 p.m. It's "protest, not charity," and the group does so with a hearty vegetarian curry or pasta served by serious activists against world hunger, poverty, and violence. Donations are greatly appreciated.

dried fungi than you can shake a Pocky stick at. Even if you're not a gourmet Chinese chef, there is enough here that's priced low enough to keep you coming back for the savings—no coupons required.

Rainbow Grocery Cooperative
1745 Folsom St.
(415) 863-0620
www.rainbowgrocery.org

Rainbow has a lot going for it—organic produce, worker-owned labor policies, and a sharp, liberal, political edge. But when it comes to saving money, the enormous serve-yourself, bulk-bin aisles are a great place to get just the right amount of dried cranberry beans, amaranth flour, nutritional yeast, trail mix, Japanese pickled plums, or about a zillion other organic, good for you, and good for the world items that you need, without paying extra (or using a boatload of packaging). Locavores can go wild, as bulk-bin labels tell you not just how much it costs per pound but also about what's in it and from where it's sourced. Extra change stays in your pocket if you bring your own bags, plastic containers, and bottles in which to carry it all home. Though Rainbow recently did away with its 20 percent–off phone book coupons (boo!), check their website for monthly deals up to 10 percent off when bringing in a receipt from another local co-op.

Sunset Supermarket
2425 Irving St.
(415) 682-3738

If mammoth local grocery store Safeway sold Asian goods and cut its prices by about two-thirds, you would have this massive food-shopping mecca's expansive size and depth. All items around the perimeter—fresh deli food, meat, fish, fruits, veggies, unrecognizable sea creatures, and, yes, even some dairy—are priced way below what you'd pay at any comparable store. Even the canned goods, packaged foods, and beverages—some familiar, many worth exploring—certainly offer you enough savings to make this destination worth a trip.

Trader Joe's
401 Bay St.
(415) 351-1013
www.traderjoes.com

Notable Bargain Buffets

Goat Hill Pizza, 300 Connecticut St.; (415) 641-1440; http://goathill .com; Mon, 5 to 10 p.m. All the pizza and salad you can ingest for $9.95 is wheeled around on carts like dim sum, hot and with a cornmeal crust. Kids ages 6 to 12 eat for just $6.

India Clay Oven, 2436 Clement St.; (415) 751-0505; http://india clayoven.com; open daily 11:30 a.m. to 2:30 p.m. Lunchtime lights up at this entirely huge selection of chicken, lamb, fish, and vegetarian Indian specialties for $9.95.

Tonga Room, 950 Mason St.; (415) 772-5278; www.tongaroom.com; Wed through Fri, 5 to 7 p.m. Technically this is a happy hour, and there is a one-drink Hawaiian cocktail minimum. But the $9.50 dinner-hour buffet is too large to be ignored, erupting with spare ribs, vegetable chow mein, pork buns, pot stickers, and the like. Not for the faint of grease.

Via Goa, 2420 Lombard St.; (415) 440-2600; open daily 11:30 a.m. to 2:30 p.m. Via Goa offers the only Goan cuisine in the Bay Area, and what better way to try this unique Portuguese-influenced, seafood-heavy fare then buffet style? At $8.99 a person, Via Goa is as easy on the wallet as it is on the stomach.

You hate it because it's a national chain, you love it because it has outstanding organic pizza for just 4 bucks—either way, you're here all the time. Parking is often a nightmare, but once you get inside, this is a dream filled with gourmet goodies, snack foods, sweets, and household items that are excellent buys, and most are pretty dang high in quality. Two additional locations are at 3 Masonic Ave. (415-346-9964), and 555 9th St. (415-863-1292).

FINE **DINING** ON **A** DIME

Alamo Square Seafood Grill
803 Fillmore St.
(415) 440-2828
Prix Fixe menu available daily from 5:30 to 7 p.m.

This cute, cozy, often overlooked seafood house on an unassuming stretch of Fillmore is a great bargain just ready for the reeling. The 3-course prix fixe is $14.50. Guests have their choice of soup or salad and then receive the chef's choice of entrees—usually a seared piece of whatever recently had been swimming, prepared simply. The finale is a slab of a house-made dessert. These are top-feeding delights at bottom-feeder prices. Sweeten the deal on Monday with a half-off wine list or no corkage fee on Wednesday.

Chapeau!
126 Clement St.
(415) 750-9787
Sun through Thurs, 5 to 6 p.m.

Delectably French, deceptively elegant, this is a classy spot for European dining, and if your butt can get in the chair before the dinner rush, you can have it all at a tremendous value: a 3-course prix-fixe dinner for $19. Diners tip their hat to onion soup baked with croutons and Emmental, roasted pork loin with French green lentils and caramelized apples, and vividly memorable classic French profiteroles. Served with precision and professionalism from a deeply caring husband-and-wife team, this is an affordable elegant evening meal at about two-thirds the usual cost.

The City Dish
www.sfcitydish.com

Kevin Blum is your host to this weekly e-mail list serving outstanding and ever-changing restaurant deals. Get on the inside track for free appetizers, buy-one-get-one-free offers, cheap drinks, and more from good places that he can cajole into a group discount. Best of all, it costs nothing to get on the mailing list, and there's no coupons to tote. For nearly every offer, just say you saw it on the City Dish. Ka-ching!

Dine About Town
www.dineabouttown.com
Jan

The San Francisco Convention and Visitors Bureau is always striving to keep SF's elite culinary houses on the menu. During the long, cold, post-holiday month when restaurant business is traditionally slow, the CVB convinces 100 or so of the town's favorite high-class eateries to compose special 3-course prix-fixe menus. For $21.95 at lunch and $31.95 at dinner, pinkie-out, penny-pinching eaters can get some real bang for their buck, particularly when you consider that many participating restaurants sell a single entree for about the same price. If you've always wanted to try Rubicon or the Acme Chophouse, this is one of the most affordable ways to dig in.

Home
2100 Market St.
(415) 503-0333
www.home-sf.com
Daily, 5 to 6 p.m.

The Catch: No substitutions are allowed.

You'd be hard-pressed to find a better early-bird dining value anywhere else in the city—3 courses for $10.99. As if 3 generous courses of hardcore comfort food weren't enough to feed the Castro dweller's heart and stomach, the restaurant throws in a glass of house wine for good measure. There are rules, however. Diners must absolutely be seated and ordering before 6 p.m., so no blowing in at the last minute. And the menu is always chef's choice, be it cauliflower soup, a pulled pork sandwich, and strawberry rhubarb crisp, or iceberg wedge, meat loaf, and sorbet. Come to Home for a hair of the dog that bit you on Sunday, where $8 bottomless mimosas flow from 10 a.m. to 3 p.m. (2-hour maximum).

Job Corps Advanced Culinary Academy Fine Dining Restaurant
Building 368, 9th Street and Avenue C, Treasure Island
(415) 277-2370
Tues through Thurs, noon seating only

The Catch: Reservations are strongly encouraged.

If you're willing to be the subject of some academic study, this is one of the most delicious ways to do it that we can think of. Advanced students

Thai Temple: It's What's for Brunch

Sure, it's not exactly fine dining, but **Berkeley's Sunday Thai Temple Brunch** is a spectacle for the eyes and stomachs that is not to be missed. Thai-tradition Buddhist monastery by week, Sun from 10 a.m. to 1 p.m. finds the temple's back courtyard transformed into a bustling Thai food bazaar packed with hungry (and often hungover) crowds of all kinds. Slurp down creamy Thai ice teas and coffees filled to the brim for only $1, and share heaping plates of pad thai and crispy rolls for $4 to $6 at community tables (grab seats where you can!). To keep the purchasing process speedy, patrons first head to the cashier's table to exchange their dollars for golden tokens. These shiny bad boys are quite literally your tokens to a belly both happy and full. Thai Temple Brunch is a short 5-minute walk from the Ashby BART station, so when you've had enough of the noodles and people watching you can browse the aisles of Ashby's weekend flea market before catching your train back home. Get in on the action at 1911 Russell St., Berkeley; (510) 849-3419; www.watmongkolberkeley.com.

of this Job Corps program are being trained to work as cooks and servers in restaurants and the hospitality industry, and they need diners to complete their experience. For $13, those with time to lunch with a view on Treasure Island will have the booty of a white-tablecloth dining experience and $13 prix fixe menu for a song. The preparation of the food is a learning experience as well, but it almost always ranges from pretty good to excellent. The bargain, however, is consistently sublime.

Millennium Restaurant

580 Geary St.
(415) 345-3900
www.millenniumrestaurant.com
Convert a Carnivore Night: second Wed of the month

The Catch: The discount does not apply to alcohol.

It's a genius scheme, really. Vegetarians and vegans are asked to bring their flesh-eating friends in for dinner one night a month to feed them the likes

Meals on Wheels: The City's Gourmet To-Go

Gourmet **food trucks** are blowing up nationwide—and San Francisco is at the heart of the drive-by street-food renaissance. This ain't your old-fashioned bread truck, neither—these souped-up yum-mobiles offer bites that fill your tummy and foodie soul without emptying your pockets. Follow them on Twitter, spot them from your upstairs window and post in the park, or race your coworkers down the stairs for the fleeting neighborhood stopover of your favorite eatery before it drives away.

Chairman Bao Bun Truck, http://twitter.com/chairmantruck. Chinese steamed buns to warm you up on one of those foggy SF days.

Crème Brûlée Cart, http://twitter.com/cremebruleecart. Quickly becoming a cult classic, crunch the sugar top of these delectable (and original) creamy cups to your heart's content.

Crepes a Go Go, http://twitter.com/crepesagogo. Sweet and savory French-style pancakes galore.

Cupkates, http://cupkatesbakery.com, http://twitter.com/cupkates truck. For the sweet-lover, "kates" won't disappoint.

El Tonayense, www.eltonayense.com. One of the best taco trucks in town.

Evil Jerk Cart, http://twitter.com/EVILJERKCART. Fiery-hot Jamaican jerk delights.

Kitchenette, http://twitter.com/kitchenettesf. Precious, gourmet, and irresistible—the menu changes daily and is based on whatever's fresh and available. Grab some Kitchenette when and where you can.

Little Green Cyclo, www.littlegreencyclo.com, http://twitter.com/lilgreencyclo. Delish and fresh Vietnamese sandwiches to-go.

Magic Curry Cart, www.magiccurrykart.com, http://twitter.com/magiccurrykart. The name says it all.

Señor Sisig, www.senorsisig.com/, http://twitter.com/senorsisig. Filipino-style tacos and burritos. Mmm-mm good.

Seoul on Wheels, www.seoulonwheels.com, http://twitter.com/seoulonwheels. Seoul-ful Korean BBQ goodness.

New food trucks crop up every day. Follow them or find a new fave on http//:roaminghunger.com/sf of porcini and Anasazi bean posole with quinoa sweet potato cake, pumpkin seed emulsion, and avocado-jicama relish, and then ask the carnivores to see the light of the meat-free diet—all for 25 percent off the total food bill (entrees are usually around $20). Certainly if every meal were as tasty as that of chef Eric Tucker's, none of us would touch meat again. No matter how you stand, this exquisite, elegant, and award-winning dining destination dangles a financial incentive to get the doubting in to give it a try, and the whole table can benefit from the experience.

2223 Market Restaurant
2223 Market St.
(415) 431-0692
www.2223restaurant.com
Tues

Whereas most entrees run upward of $20 at this well-healed Castro eatery, on 12 Buck Tuesday the tie knot loosens, and a special menu features all entrees for just $12 and starters for $6. Yum out to the likes of achiote pork loin with queso fresco *papusa,* black bean chili, and fried plantains, or Southern fried chicken nestled next to smashed buttermilk potatoes and slaw. The menu changes seasonally, emphasizes what's fresh and local, supports sustainably farmed ingredients, and uses hormone- and antibiotic-free protein sources—yet more reasons to feel good about eating here and saving a few bucks.

Zazie
941 Cole St.
(415) 564-5332
www.zaziesf.com

If you're splurging, this is a great little neighborhood French place to do it in, and you needn't be an early bird for a bite of this worm. A 3-course dinner is $19.50. Cozy, home-style cooking like mussels in white wine and garlic, followed by fish soup Provençal, and finished with crème brûlée—it's a delicious side stuffer (and a great way to plump up your date). The best part is that this special is available all night, every evening—a rarity in low-price fine dining. And, for our personal favorite, head to Zazie for the best brunch in town. True, you've got to brave the crowd, but outdoor seating with precious (and filling!) gourmet breakfast offerings makes this well worth the wait and the cheddar from your coffers.

DRINKS:
CHEAP BUZZ

"What I like to drink most is wine that belongs to others."

—DIOGENES

If we've learned anything, it's that free booze is the best booze, with the cleanest flavor and the most lingering effects. Some of us may be charming enough to get a cocktail or two purchased for us now and again, but that's an unreliable strategy, often leading to compulsory small talk with unwanted suitors. Remain charming when in a bar-type atmosphere, but keep this toolbox of free and low-cost beverage opportunities up your sleeve. At these prices, you can even afford to impress your boozing compatriots and cover the next round. Or not. Either way, the spirit of a low-price cocktail sliding down your gullet will move you.

HAPPY **HOURS**

The Attic
3336 24th St.
(415) 643-3376
Daily happy hour, 5 to 7:30 p.m.

A mere $2.50 will buy you a draft beer, a well martini (if you dare), or a well manhattan or cosmo. And while it might not be the most nutritionally sound choice, you would not be the first to rely upon the overflowing bowls of Goldfish crackers as dinner. It's dark enough in here, however, to pretend that you're someplace more divey or more posh, depending on the things you need to tell yourself.

Bean Bag Cafe
601 Divisadero St.
(415) 563-3634

The Catch: Warning: cash only.

Known for its reasonably priced breakfast plates, sandwiches, smoothies, and quick cups of coffee to stay or to go, the real gem of this corner cafe on Divis is its ridiculously cheap happy hour beers—and perhaps the longest happy hour in town (3 to 10 p.m. daily). With beers only $2.50 (plus tax), you could drink here comfortably from daytime 'til closing. And we're not talking Bud Light or Pabst Blue Ribbon, here—Bean Bag's happy hour specials are local microbrew faves like Lagunitas or classic good beers like Stella Artois. De-lish.

Blur
1121 Polk St.
(415) 567-1918
Weekdays, 4 to 6 p.m.

Oh, pay ye shall for these fancy house libations—10 bucks or more for crazy concoctions like the Blurry Dog—vodka, sake, and grapefruit juice poured strong enough to fulfill the bar's namesake. And how does this affect you? In the early-evening hours Blur offers the entire bar menu of tipplers at 2 drinks for the price of just 1. Bring a friend and you'll feel like a big spender—at half price.

Dalva
3121 16th St.
(415) 252-7740
Daily happy hour, 4 to 7 p.m.

The after-work/after-class crowd would agree: Domestic beer, house-made sangria, and well drinks for under 3 bones is a total steal, particularly when it positions you nearby so many cheap taquerias for dinner. This is a neighborhood favorite, and these early-evening hours make it an affordable way to entertain even the cheapest drunk.

Destino
1815 Market St.
(415) 552-4451
www.destinosf.com
Mon through Thurs, 5 to 7 p.m.

The Catch: *This is mostly a restaurant, with less than 10 seats at the bar (the only place a tightwad can logically sit without ordering food). Prepare to arrive early, stand with a drink in your hand, or possibly fight the midweek cocktail-loving crowd.*

Two-for-one mojitos—and these are goooood mojitos, too. Fresh mint, muddled to aromatic death, with the right balance of sugar, booze, and bubble. This tiny, stylish, often overlooked Castro joint knows how to pour 'em, and during these choice hours, they're all yours at bargain prices.

Drinking En Plein Air

One of the reasons people move to San Francisco is the mild climate—never too hot, rarely too cold. Sure, we've got fog and the occasional rain, but most days you can hang comfortably outside provided you've brought enough bundles. And nothing says San Francisco like drinking outside, whether you're brown-bagging it in Dolores Park or sipping slowly at one of the hot spots below in their copious outdoor seats. While these places aren't particularly cheap, they offer charming and comfortable seating en plein air that ups the value of your standard drink purchase.

El Rio, 3158 Mission St., (415) 282-3325; www.elriosf.com. With its huuuuuge outside garden that makes SF real estate moguls drool, El Rio is the perfect spot for large-group meet-ups or for an intimate rendezvous. $1 Pabst and $2 wells on Mon, and draft and wells both $3 from 5 to 8 p.m. Tues through Thurs. Sip these cheap treats in the garden and you'll never want to leave.

Jupiter, 2181 Shattuck Ave., Berkeley; (510) THE-TAPS; www.jupiter beer.com. Its location right next to the downtown Berkeley BART makes this swank brewery easy to get to—and home from—for any Bay Area voyager. With lovely terraced seating, house-made hoppy brews, heat lamps, and a central fire that rages all night long, you can nurse your $4 beer here for hours upon hours before rolling yourself down the BART stairs for the quick ride home.

Revolution Cafe, 3248 22nd St.; (415) 642-0474. Run—don't walk—to get here, as the seats are often full. But with outdoor heaters and live music, Revolution Cafe is the perfect early-evening, relaxed drinking spot; it's well worth waiting on the sidewalk to swipe up a seat.

Zeitgeist, 199 Valencia St.; (415) 255-7505; www.zeitgeistsf.com. Biker bar turned mainstream, this grimy bar offers the best sunny day seating, eating, and mingling the city has to offer. *Tip:* Watch out for the Tamale Lady, a San Francisco cult classic, as she wheels around her cooler to offer homemade $4 tamales that taste more like a $15 meal.

Elbo Room
647 Valencia St.
(415) 552-7788
www.elbo.com

This Mission favorite offers tons of weekly and monthly music and dancing extravaganzas (like Soul Night one Sat a month and Dubb Mission every Sun evening), but it also provides a tried-and-true, dimly lit, hipster bar scene. Prices vary, and there's often a cover price for the upstairs music, but the secret to a cheap night out at the Elbo Room is their $2 tall boys. Drink up fast so these suckers don't get too warm, and enjoy the lively atmosphere sans the overpriced libations.

540 Club
540 Clement St.
(415) 752-7276
www.540-club.com
Daily happy hour, 4 to 7 p.m.

In addition to the daily early-evening happy hour, there are two nights that are tough to ignore at this out-of-the-way Richmond District haunt. Mon night features $1 well drinks from 10 p.m. to midnight, and on Tues, during the same prime-time slot, one pays just $2 for martinis, lemon drops, man-hattans, and the like. *Tip:* Sign on to the mailing list via the website and you'll be in the know when it's free taco night or trivia night with prizes, and you'll hear about other great events at this comfy, fun, and hip hangout.

Holy Cow
1535 Folsom St.
(415) 621-6087
www.theholycow.com

Never having to pay a cover charge is a very good thing. Some say that a room brimming with Top 40 hits and Stepford-looking blonde women "slumming" in the Big City on a weekend ain't bad either. The pure holiness of Holy Cow lies in the fact that the shortest path between you and a cocktail is the cheap one, and here no tightwad will be disappointed. Thurs features dollar wells and Buds from 9 to 11:30 p.m. Fri features half-price drinks for just one golden hour—9 to 10 p.m. Sat offers the same deal, along with some potent $3 specialty house cocktails.

Home Restaurant

2032 Union St.
(415) 931-5006
www.home-sf.com
Daily, 4 to 8 p.m.

While the Castro location of Home is the place for a well-priced meal, its cousin in the north of the city on Union Street has more of a sports bar and drinking vibe, and as such, it's a great place to kick off an early evening and keep a few dollars in your pocket (no easy feat in this neighborhood). Two-for-one drinks are offered daily from 4 to 8 p.m. And while the same mac-n-cheese and banana pudding is on both Home menus, the bar here is a separate entity, so the thirsty are most welcome without the need to order food.

Pacific Cafe

7000 Geary Blvd.
(415) 387-7091

Fresh, comfortable, unfussy seafood dishes are priced well and include soup or salad and a starter—but the no-reservations policy wins its way to the cheapskate's heart through the liver: free wine while you wait. The complementary white wine flows fast and furious when the line gets going, which is nearly anytime around a mealtime. The longer you wait, the less you'll care you're waiting.

Wine Country:
Free Tastings

The only drawback in going wine tasting in Napa and Sonoma Counties is the need for a reliable designated driver after your day sloshed with a good amount of delicious, robust Zinfandels and Gewürztraminers. The positive aspects deeply weight the scale, and this is a quintessential way to spend a Northern California afternoon just an hour or so north of San Francisco. True penny-pinchers will want to bring along their own bottled water, bread, cheese, and fruit (and in summer, add a hat and some serious sunscreen to your packing list). Many places charge just a few dollars for tastings, and most will allow you to apply that money to purchases. But if you're looking to taste the sweetest, freest fruit on the vine, here is a listing of those that will allow you to taste for nothing, and you won't even have to mash grapes for the privilege. Note that most wineries in Napa have a bigger name and a bigger tourist draw, hence they are more likely to charge for the privilege of the taste. Avoiding the crowds also means avoiding the $3 to $10 "glass" fees of the larger vineyards.

Alexander Valley Vineyards, 8644 CA 128, Healdsburg; (707) 433-7209; www.avvwine.com

Cline Cellars, 24737 Arnold Dr. (CA 121), Sonoma; (707) 940-4030, (800) 546-2070; www.clinecellars.com

Field Stone Winery, 10075 CA 128, Healdsburg; (707) 433-7266; www.fieldstonewinery.com

The Toronado Pub
47 Haight St.
(415) 863-2276
www.toronado.com
Daily, 11:30 a.m. to 6 p.m.

This bar has many great things going for it: a tremendous beer selection of dozens of the best brews made anywhere in the world, for one. A great,

Fritz Winery, 24691 Dutcher Creek Rd., Cloverdale; (707) 894-3389; www.fritzwinery.com

Frog's Leap, 8815 Conn Creek Rd., Rutherford; (800) 959-4704; www.frogsleap.com

Hop Kiln Winery, 6050 Westside Rd., Healdsburg; (707) 433-6491; www.hopkilnwinery.com

And for free snacks . . .

Sonoma Cheese Factory, 2 Spain St., Sonoma; (707) 996-1931; www.sonomajack.com. Situated right on the main artery of beautiful Sonoma Square, this is one of the best (and least expensive) places to pick up picnic supplies in a convenient locale—tote a blanket and you can even have your picnic right here in the park. However, visitors are cordially invited to try before they buy, and while the cheese samples of various flavors of Monterey Jack are tiny, they are plentiful, savory, filling, and unmonitored. Have your fill of Pepper Jack and pesto Jack and dozens more before buying a thing. You might only require the bread, wine, and sausage when you're through.

Viansa Winery and Italian Marketplace, 25200 Arnold Dr., Sonoma; (707) 935-4700; www.viansa.com. Here you can dip pretzels in more varieties of mustard than you can shake an olive-tapenade-covered-cracker at. The wine is so-so, but the jars of Cal-Med snack tastes— jams, chocolate sauces, condiments as interesting and as diverse as the *terroir*—are worth a stop for lining the gullet on your way to taste wine for the day.

laid-back, Haight locale, for two. And for low-rent drinkers with time on their hands, a daily $2.50 pint special that not only starts in the a.m. but also lasts for hours and hours and is a tremendous bargain when you factor in the quality. Sure, there are pints of PBR to be had for cheaper. But when you crave a real beer from Ireland, Germany, or Seattle, this is a hop-lover's hitching post.

BREWERY & **DISTILLERY** TOURS

Anchor Brewing Company Tour
1705 Mariposa St.
(415) 863-8350
www.anchorbrewing.com/about_us/tourinfo.htm

The Catch: Reservations far in advance are absolutely required.

The only thing better than seeing how San Francisco's favorite beer is made is the generous free tasting of beer products at the end of your tour. A totally unique, delicious, and refreshing SF beer-related experience, from grain to wert to bottle, this is a great way to learn a bit of the city's history through hops. Children are welcome on the free tour (though of course tasting is available only to an age-appropriate audience). Tours fill up months in advance and are offered once daily, so book far ahead to ensure there's a tasting glass with your name on it.

Pyramid Alehouse, Brewery, and Restaurant Tours
901 Gilman St., Berkeley
(510) 528-9880
www.pyramidbrew.com
Free tours and pours daily at 4 p.m.

The Berkeley alehouse of this popular Seattle label offers free, drop-in tours and information on its brewery, plenty of time for question and answers, and other communications outreach ploys for the public. They are fully aware, however, that nothing says lovin' like a fresh pour from the tap, so every hour-long walk-through and how-to has the follow-through of sweet, delicious, free beer. Those under age 21 will enjoy the soda samplings of the house brand, Thomas Kemper. If you're feeling flush in the face and in the pockets, consider staying for standard but scrumptious brewery fare.

St. George Spirits/Hangar One Tasting Room

2601 Monarch St. (at Alameda Point), Alameda
(510) 769-1601
www.stgeorgespirits.com

Visiting our local distillery of single malt whiskey, the popular Hangar One vodka, and eclectic Aqua Perfecta eau de vie concentrated liquors in wild flavors is worth the $10 splurge, when you consider that it's a whole afternoon of fun and about four shots of booze. Call to check the seasonal tasting-room hours. Enhance the enjoyment of the great nautical outdoors by taking the Alameda Ferry from the SF Ferry Building, then learn about the process of distilling fine spirits and taste away. Groups of 10 or more get seated in a private room with one of the best views of San Francisco out there—and at no charge.

Takara Sake

708 Addison St., Berkeley
(510) 540-8250
www.takarasake.com
Daily, noon to 6 p.m.

The floors are recycled lumber, the tile is composed of recycled bottles, and the look of this massive space is more gallery than brewery. No matter how you slice it, this elegant environment is still paying out with free sake samples and a bit of information on how this rice wine has been brewed for thousands of years. Note that there is also a sake museum on-site; you are free to tour it while you swirl the contents of your glass.

BEAUTY SERVICES:
FREE STYLE

"The problem with beauty is that it's like being born rich and getting poorer."

—JOAN COLLINS

It's amazing how many hair salons, spas, and massage centers have a hoity-toity British accent, sometimes even a fake one, on their outgoing voice mail. Why? Because the world of beauty and physical maintenance has come to be seen as an element of the rich and famous, an indulgence, a high-class and often high-priced affair. But as we tightwads can attest, the latter qualification need not always be the case. Grooming and personal hygiene needn't scratch your pocketbook past skin deep. If you know where to look and have some flexibility with your schedule and your desired results, many fine local professionals can keep you looking stunning without the sting of what most are shelling out for that fresh-from-the-spa glow. Dig deep, dive in, and get more thrive for your dime.

HAIR & **SPA** SERVICES

Alexander G.
3115 Clement St.
(415) 876-4688
www.alexanderg.com

Exact policies are pretty amorphous, but interested individuals can sign up for the models list for some kind of hair style change, either a few weeks or a few months in the future, depending on your hair type, what kind of cut you'd like to have, and the type of demonstration the salon would like to perform. The best part? Cuts cost no more than $20.

Bayview Barber College
4912 3rd St.
(415) 822-3300
www.bayviewbarbercollege.com

Priding itself on turning out highly skilled students, this learning institution schools its graduates in the arts of cutting hair, scalp treatments, hair relaxing, weaves, and other tools, with a particular emphasis on African-American clientele and hair.

Beauty Bar

2299 Mission St.
(415) 285-0323
www.thebeautybar.com
Thurs through Sat, 7:30 p.m. to midnight

The Catch: *You need a $10 drink purchase to snag the freebie.*

This West Coast outpost of the national bar chain has a shtick that works: free, drunken nail care amidst cocktails kitschy and strong. Simply order the mysteriously green Prell, the deceptively undumb Platinum Blonde, or any of the house specialties, sip away, and some chick will file your daggers and slap on a coat of polish. Don't expect the greatest 'cure of your life, mind you, as you're just a part of the ambience and scenery. However, as an addendum to a raucous night on the town, it's not a bad bonus.

Blade Runners Hair Studio

1792 Haight St.
(415) 751-1723
http://bladerunnershairstudio.com
Mon

Apprentice stylists need heads to roll around, and if you call and leave your name, phone number, and hair type, they will decide if and when they're going to roll with yours. This Upper Haight salon is usually quite chic, with a reputation for excellence, and this weekly discount styling (haircuts for $15, color for $30) can be a great way to let its ambience rub off on you for a fraction of the regular cost.

Carleton Hair International

865 Market, Suite C28A, San Francisco Center
(415) 495-8300
Mon and Thurs, 11 a.m.

Call the salon anytime to sign up for these seriously cut-rate services from experienced stylists in a posh setting—$20 haircut, color starting at $25. Most weeks, they do 2 learning sessions for which they need volunteer, hair-growing heads to practice new looks and techniques.

Cinta Salon
23 Grant Ave., #2
(415) 989-1000

Ten-dollar haircuts, or $20 for a color and $35 for highlights, based on current need. Don't expect to just call up and make an appointment when you want it, but applicants looking to add a little sizzle to their look at this posh museum of style can drop by to have their locks investigated for a consultation, and then wait on the model list until their services are needed.

Dipietro Todd
177 Post St., 2nd floor
(415) 693-5549 (model hotline)
http://dipietrotodd.com
Mon, 8:45 to 9 a.m. or 1 to 1:15 p.m.

Drop by this stylish, Downtown salon in person on a Monday to show off your locks and consult with a student stylist during the hours above. Haircuts are $15; color starts at $20. Appointments will be scheduled on an individual basis, depending on the salon's need at the time. You will be attended to by an experienced student stylist, but all services are supervised by senior staff. You'll come out smelling like a rose for a song.

Edo Salon
601 Haight St.
(415) 861-0131
www.edosalon.com

Models-to-be should drop by anytime and express their interest in a new future 'do. If the stylists are seeking your type, they will call you to set something up for one of their monthly demonstration cuts for $10 or less. Forget this as a resource for a time-sensitive styling, but it could be a nice surprise if your needs coincide.

Elevations Salon and Cafe
451 Bush St.
(415) 392-2969
www.elevationsalon.com

Call to inquire about the current need for models for the on-site hair-cutting classes, but essentially, here's the drill: It takes 2 hours, and models must come by the salon/cafe for an initial consultation to show their hair length and type and to discuss what kind of new 'do they're looking for. This beautiful, upscale enterprise is huge, packed with art, and a bit of a scene unto itself. Modeling for Elevations is a good way to get a taste of it all for roughly the price of one of the organic salads and a latte from the house cafe.

Festoon Salon
9 Claude Ln.
1401 Martin Luther King Jr. Way, Berkeley
(888) 357-2566
www.festoonsalon.com

The Catch: A fee is charged. Haircuts take 2 to 3 hours; 2 to 4 hours for color. Gratuities are not included, and 48 hours notice of a cancellation is required.

To apply to be a hair model, fill out the website form every 3 months, after which time all applications are discarded. Students book a month in advance, so it can take a while to get an appointment. But once you're in, you're gorgeous for a whole lot less: $15 to $25 for a haircut, and coloring starting at $20.

Gina Kahn Salon/Yosh for Hair
173 Maiden Ln.
(415) 989-7704
www.ginakhan.com

In addition to a regular schedule of low-priced modeling opportunities for cut and color, there are also substantial special offers on their website that every style-conscious penny-pincher should be aware of, such as free hair treatments or complimentary nail service with the purchase of a regular cut and color. The offerings change frequently; check for what's on right now.

Goldstar Events Newsletter
www.goldstarevents.com

An excellent free subscription service for half-price deals on massage and spa therapies from the city's top salons. See page 29 for more about this service's offerings.

International Academy of Precision Haircutting
638 Minna St.
(415) 934-9204

Sure, the $21 cut is hardly a giveaway. But the beauty of having your cut, color, or perm done here is that the person you're trusting to make you look good actually has the chops to do the job. Students are already licensed, practicing professionals just brushing up with a few classes to heighten and brighten their skills. The heads they work on will sparkle with that touch of professionalism that only experience can bring, and the styles will be what's hot on the hair horizon. Call for an appointment anytime classes are in session.

International College of Cosmetology
1224 Polk St.
(415) 931-6333, (415) 931-6363
Drop-ins welcome Mon through Sat, 8:30 a.m. to 5 p.m.

The Catch: A low fee is charged for work done by students. Plan to spend more time here than you would at your corner salon, but the financial savings are a good incentive.

This large Vietnamese-American school of cosmetology has two locations, allowing them to double-down on the amount of skilled beauty practitioners on both sides of the bay who need bodies to practice on. You get discounted spa services: Prices start at just $4 for a shampoo, $7 for a cut, $4 for a manicure, and facials for $20. Waxing and more detailed services are also available. A second location is at 3701 International Blvd., Oakland (510-261-8256).

Mara's Salon
112A Gough St.
(415) 552-5363 (hair and tanning)
(415) 368-7917 (nails and waxing)
www.marassalon.com

The Catch: First-time customer discounts only.

In addition to the 20 percent discount on all services (including hair, nails, waxing, and tanning) for first-time clients, this salon offers deals for the white and pasty: 2 weeks of unlimited time on the tanning bed for just $45.

If you refer a friend, you both get 20 percent off of any full-priced tanning package.

Moler Barber College
64 6th St.
(510) 621-6802
Drop-ins Tues through Fri, 9:30 a.m. to 4:30 p.m.; Sat, 10:30 a.m. to 4:30 p.m.

Like most barbershops, women may want to steer clear of this venue unless they just need a quick trim or desire a short, clean-cut 'do. Guys seeking the basics, however, have it made in the shade. In just 10 or 15 minutes, they can get the basic student haircut for $7. No appointments are necessary or given.

Mr. Pinkwhistle
580 Bush St.
(415) 989-7465

Informal and easygoing, this salon with the best name ever invites potential models to pop in anytime for a consultation with the stylist on staff and to make a future appointment for a new look. They seem to use a good amount of models on a regular basis, but their needs are always in flux. Only $20 for cuts and $20 for color.

San Francisco Barber College
64 6th St.
(415) 621-6802
Wed, 8:30 a.m.

Men start lining up at 7:15 in the morning for the limited seating of these $8 no-frills cuts. While there's no official policy that women can't/won't be chosen as models, don't expect to hold on to those lengthy tresses if you make it to the chair.

San Francisco Institute of Esthetics and Cosmetology
1067 Folsom, Suite 200
(415) 355-1734
www.sanfranciscoinstitute.com

Sure, that person wielding shears by your ears is in the learning stage, but all spa services are instructor supervised. The cost savings for you can be tremendous: $20 haircut and style, $40 for color, plus body scrubs, facials, waxing, etc.—some at about half the price of what you'd expect to pay elsewhere. Some services, such as manicures, cost about the same as they do elsewhere, but take twice as long, so be sure to leave extra room in your schedule for the learning curve.

Stephen Saiz Salon

166 Geary St.
(415) 398-2345
http://stephensaizsalon.com
Tues

The Catch: *The cut is free, but this is more of a "scalpel" donation than a service. The stylists will use your hair as they see fit.*

Call and check in often to learn about what hair type they're currently seeking. If the way you're growing it is what they're looking for, you will be invited to come in and sit as a model for their cutting class for the in-house stylists held one day a week. This is one of the few salons that is up front about the fact that there is no consultation with the models. The stylists will use you as they see fit, thus you have just a vague idea of what sort of style you may end up with before the scissors fly.

Vidal Sassoon

359 Sutter St.
(415) 397-5105
Model drop-ins Thurs, 6 p.m.

The San Francisco location of this international learning mecca needs a whole host of models for various projects. Thus, they want you and your hair to drop by for a look-see on Thursday evenings (no more than 30 minutes or so) to meet with the stylists and to schedule you for the learning day that will suit you both the best. Expect the learning shampoo, cut, and style to take up to 3 hours—but hey, they don't look good unless you look good, right? Cuts are $16, color is $20—all services are cash only, gratuity not included.

Alternative Healing on the Cheap

San Francisco's known for healing varieties of all kinds—chiropractic circus yoga, regressive crystal hypnotherapy, acusound pressure, chakra cooking, Atlantean healing. In San Francisco, we've got it all. The problem is that these kind of services often cost the arm and the leg you're there to heal. Not so at these fine SF cheap-healing gems.

Alive & Well Institute of Conscious BodyWork; 1058 Redwood Hwy., Mill Valley; (415) 388-9949; www.alivewell.com/massage.htm. North across the Golden Gate Bridge is a segue to pain-free living for those who suffer from chronic back issues. Progressive, innovative practices lie at the student hands of those practicing conscious bodywork and neuromuscular reprogramming—new ideas in physical and mental treatment for difficult discomfort. Massage treatments begin at $28 for 50 minutes. Learn more about the treatment and the services offered to the general public through the institution.

American College of Traditional Chinese Medicine, 450 Connecticut St.; (415) 282-9603. Want to get needled on the cheap? Call to make an appointment at the American College of Traditional Chinese Medicine to get acupuncture and herb treatments by doctors in training on a sliding scale. Special discounts for students and seniors. After breezing out from your low-cost appointment, your chi will be humming for the rest of the day (with your wallet still comfortably filled).

Quan Yin Healing Arts Center, 965 Mission St; (415) 861-4964; www.quanyinhealingarts.com. Stop by Quan Yin to make an appointment for acupuncture, acupressure, massage, and a whole host of other healing arts that won't drain your flow (energetic or financial). Designed to bring alternative therapies to those in need, Quan Yin offers a variety of services including yoga, qi gong, and support groups for those in need of mental/physical/emotional tune-ups.

World School of Massage and Holistic Healing Arts, 401 32nd Ave.; (415) 221-2533; www.worldschoolmassage.com; Wed and Fri. You can be on the lucky receiving end of massage students in need of hands-on practice for a deep-tissue discount. Call the school to set up a late-afternoon appointment and inquire about which styles will be executed that week—shiatsu, Swedish, vibrational massage, or a panoply of others. Then let their fingers do the walking all over you on your way to relaxation. The cost is typically $40 for a 1-hour massage.

Womack's Salon Academy

598 Silver Ave.
(415) 334-7774
Drop-ins Tues, 11:30 a.m. to 3 p.m.

Seniors and retirees are especially encouraged to drop by any Tuesday for a free cut and styling, but your locks can actually make you cash at this learning institution. Cheap Bastards will earn scores of cheapie points if they do the following: Sign up to help the Womack students pass their state board exams in Fairfield. Allow a student to cut your hair for free a couple of times. Then, ride with the student to Fairfield on the day of the exam to have your hair cut in front of an audience, and earn about 100 bucks or so for your troubles. All arrangements are to be made between models and their student stylist; inquire within.

Zenzi's Cosmetology Training Center

551 Hayes St.
(415) 575-3540
www.zenzis.org
Tues through Sat

Tony Hayes Valley has been home to this equally posh learning institution in beauty education for almost 75 years. Excellent products, state-of-the-art facilities, and earnest students are the hallmark of the full range of spa services, which include everything from hair, nails, and waxing to facials and makeup application. Cuts start at $10, facials at $25, and color at $35.

MASSAGES

The Clinic at McKinnon Institute, LLC

2940 Webster St.
(510) 465-3488
www.mckinnonmassage.com

The school's professional massage services are available to the public at prices that won't rub you the wrong way—1-hour massages start at $40.

A complete toolbox of massage modalities are on hand for your relaxing pleasure, including acupressure, craniosacral, Swedish, reflexology, shiatsu, chair, pregnancy, deep tissue, and Thai massage. Call to schedule an appointment and speak with a practitioner.

Diamond Massage and Wellness Center
1841 Lombard St.
(415 921-1290
www.diamondwellness.com

The Catch: Pro bono or discounted services given only under certain circumstances.

Driven by a higher mission of community outreach and a quest for wellness and good health, these small practitioners offer financial incentives for various strata of the massage-needing public. A certain number of appointments are pro bono for qualifying recipients every month, and teachers receive a 10 percent discount at all times. Friends referring friends get a free massage. There are last-minute discounts, Web-only coupons for special services, and more. Log on to find out what's available this month.

Stacy Simons, Certified Massage Therapist
2983 Folsom St.
(415) 254-4763
www.littleepiphany.com/massage.htm
Tues and Thurs, 11 a.m.

This private individual specializing in Swedish and deep-tissue massage reserves these two time slots every week for sliding-scale clients, first come, first served. Prices start at $35. The slots usually fill up quickly. She practices at a number of locations around SF, including the Mission, Downtown, and Ocean Boulevard. Read more about her background and the community services she offers at the link above.

FAMILY RESOURCES:
OFF TO A CHEAP START

"The easiest way for your children to learn about money is for you not to have any."

—KATHARINE WHITEHORN

All parents, particularly those of newborns and preschool-age children, need help wherever they can find it. In the case of the parent looking to make every penny sing, finding these family-boosting resources can be a great challenge. San Francisco may not be an ideal village for raising kids, but hey, we've got enough in the way of low-cost health care, free and low-cost child care, and stores selling half-price clothing and equipment to give it an honest go. Save your money for where it really counts: ice-cream cones, Vegas junkets for mom and dad, and your child's fixed-rate, local state school college tuition.

GENERAL **RESOURCES**

Bananas Childcare Referral and Support
5232 Claremont Ave., Oakland
(510) 658-7353
www.bananasinc.org

With services offered in almost a dozen languages, this nonprofit agency helps connect parents with trained child care and offers a massive library, video collection, and collection of handouts on effective parenting. Their exhaustive calendar of classes and events include support groups, CPR training, and baby basics. There's a free infant and child clothing exchange, and Bananas provides direction on subsidized child care for low-income caregivers.

Berkeley Parents Network
http://parents.berkeley.edu

This collective online repository and brain trust overflows with all of the Bay Area's resources for parents, babies, kids, and families, and with more than 30,000 members there's plenty of user experience and reviews to back it up. A great resource for finding the perfect pediatrician and preschool, plus, if you want it, there's also parenting advice galore, based on the knowledge of families associated with the University of California at Berkeley.

Family Ambassador Project
(415) 682-3239

This telephone hotline helps English- and Spanish-speaking parents track down a current list of parent education and support groups, many of which are free or low cost. The hotline specializes in helping to uncover somewhat more obscure resources for all kinds of families, such as those speaking languages other than English or LGBT (lesbian, gay, bisexual, and transgender) families. Contact the project for the latest list of workshops about local resources and how to advocate for child services.

Family Paths
(800) 829-3777

Twenty-four hours a day, 7 days a week, anyone from all over the Bay Area can phone this hotline for assistance with parental stress of any kind. Topics covered and references given tend to revolve around crisis intervention, counseling, and referrals to resources for children. Family Paths also has offices now in Oakland, Hayward, and Fremont.

La Leche League
http://lllnorcal.org
(415) 320-8116

Considered to be the world's leading support organization for breast-feeding moms, La Leche League hosts free meetings twice a month in San Francisco, and more around the Bay Area. Certified and experienced lactation consultants provide support, instruction, and guidance during those early days with the hungry new baby.

Natural Resources
1367 Valencia St.
(415) 550-2611
www.naturalresources-sf.com

This prenatal and childbirth preparation center offers numerous resources for its paying clients, but it provides the following as a community service free to the public: Monthly "meet the doulas" and "meet the midwives" events connect new parents to practitioners, Bay Area Homebirth Collective events provide exposure to birthing options around the bay, DiaperDays and

Carrier Clinics offer information on the basics of choosing the best baby equipment, not to mention legal planning and even photography basics. If you can't make it to one of these free events, they also provide a readily available library of binders to help mom and dad find day care, babysitting, pediatricians, and alternative health professionals.

Nursing Mothers' Council
(650) 327-MILK
Redwood City, San Bruno, Santa Cruz
www.nursingmothers.org

Free online pamphlets, telephone consultations, breast-pump rentals, breast-feeding classes, and home visits are offered to breast-feeding moms by volunteers, with no cost obligation to the public.

Parent's Place
1710 Scott St.
(415) 359-2454
www.parentsplaceonline.org

This comprehensive family support service organization through Jewish Family and Children's Services offers sliding-scale workshops, play groups, development groups, mentoring, resources for dads, and more. They offer some of the best resources for families with special needs children, and have added a preschool preview night to help send your kid off into the world of academia on the right foot.

Postpartum Support International
(800) 944-4PPD
Daily, 9 a.m. to 9 p.m.

Callers leave their first name and a phone number, and a volunteer who has survived PPD will return the call same day. In addition to providing someone to talk to, the volunteers will refer new moms to self-help resources and a handful of low-cost professionals. The call and the service are free.

San Francisco General Women's Health Center
1001 Potrero Ave.
(415) 206-3409

The Catch: In our experience, lines are long, and those seeking information can expect lengthy delays.

This public hospital owned by the city offers its services to all residents, with free or low-cost services based on individual eligibility. No one is turned away, and services are offered in English, Spanish, and Chinese.

SFkids
http://sfkids.org

One of the most comprehensive online resources for San Francisco families, the emphasis here is on enrichment, activity, and entertainment but with your budget in mind. These guys acknowledge that San Fran is not the cheapest place to raise a family, and they have a massive database of ideas for outings, adventures, camps, sports, and more.

Telephone Aid in Living with Kids (TALK)
1757 Waller St.
(415) 441-KIDS
www.talklineforparents.org

The Catch: Services are free, but some require preregistration.

This organization offers a host of community services for parents at the risk of burnout, including workshops, drop-in sessions on parenting skills, substance abuse assistance, counseling, group support, and child play groups. The signature community benefit is the 24-hour crisis and counseling telephone line for parents to call for support, information, and referrals.

Safety First

San Francisco Department of Public Health's Children's Environmental Health Promotion, 1390 Market St., Suite 230; (415) 554-8930 (lead poisoning prevention), (415) 554-8930, ext. 11 (asthma information); www.sfdph.org. In an effort to raise healthy children in a city full of century-old homes, this public service says it will come to your house and help educate your family on the risks of lead poisoning in children, coordinate medical intervention in lead poisoning cases, identify lead hazards, and advise property owners (you or your landlord) on safe remediation methods. Families of asthma sufferers can also receive information on the physicality and treatment of the disease, assistance implementing environmental controls, home assessment, some free home control devices (like new air filters), and referrals to other social services.

San Francisco Police Department Child Safety Program, (415) 575-6363. Call this number and arrange a visit with a police officer to ensure that your infant car seat has been properly installed.

San Francisco Water Department, (877) 737-8297. This public utility can be difficult to navigate, but it will do free lead testing of your home water supply.

Women and Children's Health Referral Line at the Department of Public Health
(800) 300-9950

This local service agency points parents toward health-care options for their children, particularly for parents who are seeking advice in disability prevention and for youngsters with special needs. While the agency's services—such as WIC, AIM, Healthy Kids, and MediCal—are of most interest to low-income families, the agency can point anyone toward low-cost clinics, classes, and other services.

Universal Home Visiting Program of the Department of Public Health

30 Van Ness Ave.
(415) 575-5727, (415) 575-5705

Regardless of income, language, or hospital affiliation, the city will send a public health nurse to your home for a free newborn and new mother exam within a week after delivery. Patients are usually referred to this program through their birthing hospital, but any citizen is welcome to call and arrange a visit postpartum.

PLAY **GROUPS** & **CLASSES**

City College of San Francisco Department of Child Development and Family Studies Parent and Infant and Parent and Child Classes

(415) 561-1921
www.ccsf.edu/Departments/Child_Development/programs.html

When the college has courses in session, it encourages parents and children—newborns to kindergarteners—to attend no-cost play groups in the child development program. Certified instructors head up these gatherings, child development students learn from the study participants, and the kids get a great play session with others their own age. Parents are often interviewed about their child and their role and may receive tips on health, safety, and daily routines. Download this semester's schedule of class times and locations.

Congregation Sha'ar Zahav

290 Dolores St.
(415) 861-6932
www.shaarzahav.org

In addition to a for-pay religious school and programs for teens, this LGBT temple in the Mission offers monthly baby meeting groups and tot Shabbat programs that invite the public to come and meet the congregation at no cost.

Congregation Sherith Israel
2266 California St.
(415) 346-1720
www.sherithisrael.org

Check the calendar for a whole month filled with meet-and-greets for babies, kids, and families. Weekly meetings of preschool kids of all ages are slated alongside moms' groups, dads' groups, baby-friendly yoga classes, music classes, tot Shabbat, and heaps more. Families of all faiths are welcome. Many gatherings are free, offer a free first visit, or are otherwise affordable to the community at large.

Golden Gate Mothers Group
www.ggmg.org

The Catch: Membership is $55 a year. Nannies and spouses are not welcome to many of the activities.

Yes, it does cost money to be a part of this club, but moms of young children get an awful lot for their dollar. In addition to the group newsletter and e-mail discussion list, there are regular monthly educational meetings, organized play groups, holiday events, welcome teas, and the like. The emphasis here is on the kids, but it's a great resource for moms during those few moments of the day when you're not on duty.

Peakaboutique's Tot Parties
1306 Castro St.
(415) 641-6192
Last Thurs of the month, 6 p.m.

This popular used children's goods store in Noe Valley invites its shoppers and its neighbors in for free wine for mom and dad, free juice for the kids, and an opportunity to foster a little bit of community around the pursuit of retail. During the summer months this event may be canceled due to travel schedules. It's a good idea to call and confirm before attending.

AFTER-SCHOOL **PROGRAMS** & **CHILD** CARE

Babysitter Exchange
www.babysitterexchange.com

Though not specific just to parents in the Bay Area, this online co-op allows parents situated near one another to meet, gain trust, and watch one another's kids—all without costing anyone a dime. You contribute time and evenings in, but you get the same in return, if you can find like-minded members of your community to share in your pursuit to get out of the house. It's a bit cumbersome to get an exchange started, but once it's up and running, this is the best thing since dinner and a movie.

Children's Council of San Francisco
445 Church St.
(415) 343-3300
www.childrenscouncil.org
Second Tues of the month, 6 to 8 p.m.

This is an opportunity to meet other parents in need of child care for a potential swapping of services, organized nanny share, or co-op. Parents from all over are welcome to attend free information workshops to learn about child-care options as well as about the legal obligations of care providers, licensing regulations for day-care operations, screening tests for potential care providers, and more. Care for children older than babies-in-arms can be arranged at least one week in advance.

Downtown Berkeley YMCA Childwatch Program, Fit Kids, and Family Night
2001 Allston Way, Berkeley
(510) 848-9622
www.baymca.org

The Catch: An extra dollar fee is added per diaper change, and parents are fined $5 for every 10 minutes they go over the 2-hour limit.

Similar to YMCA programs offered elsewhere, here the 2-hour-max Childwatch program welcomes children as young as 8 weeks and as old as 7 years. Note that other East Bay YMCAs offer additional child-care and play activities for children of all ages at significantly reduced fees.

Kidspace at the LBGT Center

1800 Market St.
(415) 865-5639
www.sfcenter.org/kidspace.php
Reservations: ariannec@sfcenter.org
Hours vary; closed Tues and Wed

Whether dad and dad or mom and mom (or sometimes, even mom and dad) are popping in for a meeting or support group, attending a social function, or just stopping in to use their laptop at Three Dollar Bill Cafe, parents will kick up their rainbow high heels to learn that free and donation-based child care and supervised group play is available by prearranged reservation for tots from infant to school age. Junior is cared for by skilled and certified educators and interacts with other kids of LGBT parents for arts and crafts, story time, dancing, etc.

Richmond YMCA Childwatch Program

360 18th Ave.
(415) 666-9622
www.ymcasf.org/Richmond
Mon through Fri, 8:30 a.m. to 12:30 p.m.; Thurs, 4:30 to 7:30 p.m.; Sat, 8:45 a.m. to 1 p.m.

In addition to low-cost before- and after-school child care, the Richmond Y offers supervised care for your child, ages 3 months to 12 years, for a maximum of 2 hours while you take a class and work out; the fee is $4 an hour. Adults must remain on premises, but with a full calendar of dance, yoga, cardio classes, and muscle conditioning, there will be plenty to do to give your body a workout and your parenting mind a break.

Note that many other YMCA branches offer inexpensive before-school, after-school, and summer camp programs as well. For more information visit www.ymcasf.org.

Secondhand Maternity-, Baby- & Kid-Supply Stores

Why pay top dollar for new clothes and toys they'll outgrow in a New York minute? Buy it used—or sell it when you're done—at any of these local retailers:

Chloe's Closet, 451 Cortland Ave. and 616 Irving St.; (415) 642-3300; www.chloescloset.com. This "best of the bay" award winner 5 years running specializes in recycled and new children's clothing, toys, gear, and games, and maternity clothing galore. The 2 locations accept different items if you're looking to cash in, so visit the website for details. Mailing list members can earn a $5 store credit for signing up, and texting Chloe at 72727 will get you a 15 percent discount valid for 30 days!

MaternityXchange.com. Locations vary. Create a free account to browse all of your maternity consignment needs, and join the mailing list to learn about their regular designer maternity clothing sales around the Bay Area.

Peekabootique, 1306 Castro St.; (415) 641-6192; www.peekaboo tiquesf.com. Nestled (ever so appropriately) in the heart of Noe Valley, they specialize in the top-of-the-line children's products, both new and gently used. If you're looking to sell your own baby stuff, call for an appointment.

Town School Clothes Closet, 1850 Polk St.; (415) 929-8019; www .townschoolclothescloset.org. Buying and selling here benefits the Town School for Boys tuition assistance program, and the store is chock full of high end items for the whole family, not just the tots!

And of course, what would any kind of shopping be without **Craigslist** and **eBay** . . .

San Francisco Beacon Initiative
1390 Market St., Suite 900
(415) 554-8990
www.sfbeacon.org

A number of after-school programs and homework-help opportunities are found at nine locations around the city.

San Francisco Recreation and Parks' Latchkey Program
(415) 715-4065
http://parks.sfgov.org

All children who are San Francisco residents in grades 1 through 5 qualify for this city-run after-school and summer camp program at deeply discounted rates, and your 6th- to 8th-grade preteens can attend the after-school leadership program. Full-day summer care programs are also offered for a fraction of what one would expect to pay at a private day-care center. The program happens at 16 different locations around SF; consult the website to find the location that's most convenient for your family as well as current registration information.

Wu Yee Children's Services
706 Mission St., 6th floor
(415) 677-0100, (415) 391-4956 (referral line)
www.wuyee.org

This is a great place for parents to learn about their child-care options. Staff members provide workshops on identifying quality child care, and they can help families determine if their income level qualifies them for defrayed child-care costs or for city or government programs. For families who qualify, Wu Yee offers its own child-care program for infants through 5-year-olds. A private preschool exists for a higher cost for ages 3 to 5. Many other child services are offered in a number of languages to help families on the grow.

KID STUFF:
BIG FUN FOR
SMALL CHANGE

*"I take my children everywhere, but they
always find their way back home."*

—ROBERT ORBEN

Why does entertaining your kids have to cost so much? It doesn't, if you're a savvy parent who knows where to find a bargain in children's entertainment. For toddler or teenager, there are about a zillion ways to amuse the whippersnappers around the bay. And while this is by no means a complete list, here are a few of the most interesting and innovative. Pack up a stack of PB&Js, and you needn't even give in to the cries of "lunch!" This is homespun fun at its best.

MUSIC & **STORY** TIME

Breakfast with Enzo
LMNO Music with Enzo Garcia
Bernal Heights Neighborhood Center
Sports Basement in the Presidio
www.enzogarcia.com
Fri and Sat, 10 a.m. to noon

The Catch: $5 or $6 depending on the location.

It's strictly BYOB at this low-cost weekend morning affair—bring your own breakfast. While you munch you will be entertained with song, rhythm, movement, and melody for infants, children, and preschoolers by this niche musician of the accordion, banjo, and song. If you like what you see during this weekend performance, you can sign up for the artist's pay session weekly meetings in small, interactive groups.

San Francisco Public Library
(415) 557-4400
www.sfpl.org (click on "Events for Kids and Families" under the Kids tab)

The events and locations change every month, but one thing is always constant: the tremendous amount of no-cost activities offered for kids from birth through their teens. From story times, sing-alongs, and baby bounces to puppet shows and Banned Books Reading Clubs for older kids, there is truly something at every city branch to stimulate the mind of children of all ages. These are your tax dollars at work, people, so be sure to crack the cover and take advantage.

RIDES, **THRILLS** & **AMUSEMENT** PARKS

Carousel in Golden Gate Park
Martin Luther King Jr. Drive and Bowling Green Drive
(415) 812-2725

Adjacent to the newly renovated Golden Gate Park Children's Playground (now called Koret Children's Quarter), this classic carved merry-go-round is a must-see tourist attraction packed with charm and nostalgia—oh, and the kids will like it, too. Calliope music, sprightly horses that bob up and down, and the much-coveted teacup seat make this a ride to remember and a great part of spending a lovely day in the park. And for the price—$1.50 for adults, 50 cents for kids ages 6 to 12—riding the carousel is worth it for the photo ops alone.

Children's Fairyland

699 Bellevue Ave., Oakland
(510) 452-2259
www.fairyland.org

For the preschool set, this magical miniland—where classic children's stories come to life alongside farm animals, storybooks, and puppet shows—is the kiddie amusement park that can kick a certain giant mouse's tail any day. Parents lounge in the shade while young explorers take on rides and plenty of safe bridges, waterways, and play structures. Best of all, it's a stunning view across Lake Merritt and an easy walk from BART. It ain't free, but your 8 bucks (free admission for children under the age of 1) buys unlimited rides, making the value giant sized.

Redwood Valley Railway

Tilden Regional Park, Berkeley
Grizzly Peak Boulevard and Lomas Cantadas Road
(510) 548-6100
www.redwoodvalleyrailway.com
Weekends, 11 a.m. to 6 p.m., year-round

This massive green space in the East Bay offers swimming at Lake Anza, the wonder of the petting zoo, the enjoyment of the carousel, and the opportunity to just roll around in the splendor. But it's the child-size steam train that young kids and train enthusiasts return to again and again for 12 minutes of steam-powered bliss. All aboard! And note that your dog can ride for free. Tickets are $2, or grab 5 for $8. Call ahead for closures in case of inclement weather.

Santa Cruz Beach Boardwalk

400 Beach St., Santa Cruz
(831) 423-5590
Closed for maintenance in early Dec and Christmas Day; otherwise open daily year-round

The only major boardwalk amusement park on the West Coast is entirely worth the beautiful drive down the PCH. It's got all the makings of the boardwalks your grandparents told you about: old-school roller coasters, fun house, Dippin' Dots (well, maybe they didn't have Dippin' Dots back then). Admission to the boardwalk is free, so you only pay for individual rides

Recreation Centers with Free Cooking Classes for Kids

With the roller coaster ride of city funding and budget cuts, programs like these can be hard to track down and even harder to keep in operation. Be sure to call or consult websites to make sure these are up and running. If they are, you'll have hit the jackpot in terms of fun, enriching stimulation for the little ones. Public programs in the city's parks focus on health and wellness, getting your kids on a health kick without them even knowing it!

Bayview Hunters Point Beacon Center, 400 Mansell St.; (415) 469-4550; www.sfbeacon.org/beaconcenters/bayview-hunterspoint/

Bernal Heights Playground and Recreation Center, 500 Moultrie St.; (415) 695-5007

Boys and Girls Clubs of San Francisco—Tenderloin Clubhouse, 115 Jones St.; (415) 351-3125

Ella Hill Hutch Community Center, 1050 McAllister St.; (415) 921-6276; http://ellahillhutchcommunitycenter.org

Gilman Playground Rec Connect, Gilman Avenue and Griffith Street; (415) 678-8007; www.hunterspointfamily.com/gilman-rec-connect/

Hayes Valley Playground, Hayes and Buchanan; (415) 554-9526; register for programs at sfreconline.org

Joseph Lee Recreation Center, 1395 Mendell; (415) 822-9040

Minnie and Lovie Ward Rec Center, Capitol and Montana; (415) 337-4710

Mission Neighborhood Centers, Inc., various locations; (415) 206-7752; www.mncsf.org

Palega Recreation Center, 500 Felton St.; (415) 468-2875

Up on Top Afterschool and Summer Program, 1187 Franklin St; (415) 225-6558; www.upontop.org

Upper Noe Recreation Center, Day and Sanchez; (415) 970-8061

(starting at $2.25 per ride). On Friday nights during the summer the Bands on the Beach event is free and open to the public.

Studio 39's Magic Carpet Ride
Pier 39, the Embarcadero

The Catch: Making the video is free; there's a steep fee to purchase a copy.

In an entirely over-touristed part of town, it's rare to find any kind of free entertainment. But when you've grown tired of listening to the seals and taking in the silver-painted street performers, this is a chance for you and yours to be the star of the show. Step in front of the blue screen, ham it up, and "fly" above the sights of SF in your own 5-minute video. If you like what you see you'll have to shell out 40 bucks to take home a copy. Don't blame us if you get suckered in. We're just letting you know that the making of the video is free.

MUSEUMS & **TOURS**

California Academy of Sciences
55 Music Concourse Dr.
(415) 379-8000
www.calacademy.org
Free every third Wed of the month

The newly renovated California Academy of Sciences is one of the most exciting and entertaining outings San Francisco has to offer. Unfortunately, you'll spend this month's rent trying to get the whole family in at one time. Thankfully the academy knows that Cheap Bastards are parents too! If you can get that third Wednesday morning off, head to the park and check out the living roof (the lush, native-species garden that carpets the academy's roof); a mesmerizing albino alligator; the fantastic aquarium, including the hands-on touching pond; the indoor rainforest; and, of course, the spectacular planetarium. Get there early as the place is packed on free days and last entry is at 4 p.m. If you're an SF resident, be sure to check their website for additional neighborhood-specific free days!

Bay Area County Fairs

These yearly kid-centric events make for a full weekend of fun that is sure to tire the young' uns out by 7 p.m. Ticket prices vary but are usually between $4 and $8, tiny ones go free; dates vary every year, usually one weekend in June, July, or August.

Contra Costa County Fair, Antioch; www.contracostafair.com

Giants County Fair, AT&T Park in San Francisco; http://sanfrancisco.giants.mlb.com

San Mateo County Fair, San Mateo; www.sanmateocountyfair.com

Alameda County Fair, Pleasanton; http://alamedacountyfair.com

Solano County Fair, Vallejo; www.scfair.com

Sonoma Marin Fair, Petaluma; www.sonoma-marinfair.org

Marin County Fair, San Rafael; www.marinfair.org

Napa County Fair, Calistoga; www.napacountyfairgrounds.com

California State Fair, Sacramento; www.bigfun.org

Sonoma County Fair, Santa Rosa; www.sonomacountyfair.com

Santa Clara County Fair, San Jose; http://thefair.org/home.cfm

Cartoon Art Museum

655 Mission St.
(415) CAR-TOON
www.cartoonart.org
One or two Sat a month, 1 to 3 p.m.

Kids ages 8 to 14 are encouraged to come learn about this exciting, kid-friendly medium one panel at a time. Topics covered include character design, storyboarding, and the creation of their own mini comic book. The calendar changes often, so call to inquire about upcoming classes. Classes and materials are free with the $5 price of museum admission. Weeklong summer camps are also offered for roughly $100 for 5 days of instruction. Registration is recommended as classes are first come, first served, and cap at 20 kids.

Fortune Cookie Factory

261 12th St., Oakland
(510) 832-5552

The Catch: A reservation is required for groups of 10 or more.

Yes, Virginia, there are other fortune cookie factories to visit in SF's Chinatown, but this is the real deal both in size and scope. It's one of the oldest, and it's the only one that can truly accommodate large groups. It's worth crossing the bridge to Oakland and paying the buck admission to have an opportunity to put your own message inside a cookie; an order of 1,000 is just $12. Your $1 admission fee includes a small bag of cookies. When with the kiddos, beware the bin of sexy R-rated fortunes!

Jelly Belly Factory Tour
1 Jelly Belly Ln., Fairfield
(800) 9-JELLYBEAN (800-953-5592)
www.jellybelly.com

One hour's drive north of San Francisco, the colorful, sweet magic happens. This mammoth jelly bean factory will not only entertain you during the totally free 40-minute walking tour, but not a single parent or child walks out without a generous bag of free candy. Pair that with all the samples given in the storefront following the tour and voilà!—high-fructose lunch. On display are excellent mosaics of Ronald Reagan, Elvis Presley, Marilyn Monroe, and other celebrity classic figures forever commemorated in the Day-Glo candy. The huge factory of brilliantly hued working turbines is truly a sight to behold.

Midweek tours, when the factory workers are actually on-site, are much, much better than the weekend video-only tours.

Worth the Trip
In an effort to boost interest in the fancy and freedom of flight, the nonprofit EAA Aviation Foundation offers children ages 8 to 17 a free flight in a small plane piloted by a credited pilot over the clouds of the Bay Area at the **Hiller Aviation Museum** at the San Carlos Airport (620 Airport Dr., San Carlos; 650-654-0200; www.hiller.org/young-eagles.shtml), about 30 minutes south of San Francisco. Your kids are welcome to earn their wings on a first come, first served basis—but get there early, as this tends to be insanely crowded, particularly in summer.

MOCHA Museum of Children's Art

538 9th St., Oakland
(510) 465-8770
www.mocha.org
Tues through Fri, 10 a.m. to 5 p.m.; Sat and Sun, noon to 4 p.m.

The Catch: *$8 drop-in fee for hands-on creativity (no charge for the adults), but entrance to the gallery is free.*

Get your 18-month-old (or older) interested in art and expression at this massive workshop space ready to accept paint-splattered creativity on a drop-in basis. Go with the museum's weekly theme or simply let your youngsters' imagination run wild—either way, for less than it would cost you to take the kids to the movies, they can unleash their little artist inside. While you're there, plant the seeds of art appreciation in the adorable, child-powered, and surprisingly potent exhibit hall.

Musee Mecanique

Pier 45, Shed A (at the end of Taylor Street)
(415) 346-2000
www.museemechanique.org

Laughing Sal, an 8-foot mechanical puppet behind glass from the turn of the 20th century, is downright creepy as she cackles away. But this entirely unique arcade of automated flip books, hand-powered robots, and entire carnivals made from lit-up toothpicks is completely fascinating and a wonderful historical window into how people got their jollies along the waterfront before the advent of electronic video games (though a few of those are on hand, too). This is absolutely a must-see, not just for kids but even for adults. It's worth braving the tourism and traffic of Fisherman's Wharf—yes, it's that good. Best of all, it costs nothing to walk in the door and pocket change to make the magic happen. And if you time it right, you can enjoy the player pianos on someone else's quarter.

Randall Museum

199 Museum Way
(415) 554-9600
www.randallmuseum.org
Tues through Sat, 10 a.m. to 5 p.m.

In addition to being an extremely cool museum geared toward younger kids with a great playground and lots of hands-on activities, Randall Museum offers regular and drop-in arts and craft classes in clay, woodworking, magic lessons, and heaps more by the barrel. Admission to the museum is free; most classes are $4. Kids are also welcome to feed the critters in the small animal petting zoo or operate the impressive model train city, both activities on Saturday only.

San Francisco Maritime National Historical Park
National Park Service
Hyde Street Pier (Hyde and Beach Streets)
(415) 447-5000
www.nps.gov/safr/local/calendar.html
9:30 a.m. to 5:30 p.m. June through Aug; 9:30 a.m. to 5 p.m. Sept through May

The Catch: *Kids under 16 are free, but everyone else has to fork over $5 for a ticket (valid for 7 days).*

While there are some hefty fees for touring the fleet of ancient shipping vessels and the submarine, the USS *Pampanito,* the Maritime offers up a tremendous amount of free, nautically themed events of interest to older kids with a lust for the pirate's life and an interest in SF's history as a port city. Particularly in summer, programs like Sea Chantey Sing-Alongs, a tour of the collection's small crafts via boat ride to Alameda, bird-watching tours, crafts, and ships' radio demonstrations abound. Check the calendar and ahoy, ahoy.

San Francisco Zoo
1 Zoo Rd.
(415) 753-7080
www.sfzoo.org
Daily, 10 a.m. to 5 p.m.

The Catch: *Regular admission is steep, but SF residents enjoy substantial discounts: $9 for adults, $5.50 for kids, and free for those under 3.*

The largest zoo in Northern California, it's a sure bet for the little ones. Chances are you know what to expect, but check the website for inexpensive weeklong summer camps.

CLASSES & **ACTIVITIES**

Shan-Yee Poon Ballet School
403 Arguello Blvd.
(415) 387-2695
www.poonballet.com

Ever wonder what your toddler would look like in a tutu? How about your teenager in tap shoes? Parents are welcome to this serious dance school's

---

Recreation Centers with Free Arts & Crafts for Kids

Let your school-age Picassos unleash their right brain at the following locations. Students needn't bring anything but their imagination. Schedules change often; it's a good idea to call and confirm. Programs, schedules, and locations change frequently. For an exhaustive list and to register for programs visit http://sfreconline.org.

Boedekker Park, 240 Eddy; (415) 292-2019

Christopher Playground, 5210 Diamond Heights Blvd.; (415) 695-5000

Douglass Playground, 26th Street and Douglass; (415) 695-5017

Eugene Friend Rec Center, 270 6th St.; (415) 554-9532

Gilman Playground, Gilman Avenue and Bill Walsh Way; (415) 467-4566

Grattan Playground, 1180 Stanyan; (415) 753-7039

Hamilton Recreation Center, 1900 Geary Blvd.; (415) 292-2008

Hayes Valley Playground, Hayes and Buchanan; (415) 554-9526

Helen Wills Playground, Broadway and Larkin; (415) 359-1281

Joe DiMaggio Playground, 651 Lombard; (415) 391-0437

Julius Kahn Playground, W. Pacific Avenue and Spruce; (415) 292-2004

Tenderloin Recreation Center, 570 Ellis; (415) 753-2761

Youngblood Coleman Playground, Mendell and Galvez; (415) 695-5005

---

frequent orientation programs, and their children are welcome to test out a class for free before committing to a hefty prepaid schedule. Voted best dance school in 2010's Best of the Bay, in addition to ballet the school offers jazz, tap, and more to the lithe and graceful. Be careful. Your kid may just love it.

Tiny Tots, a project of San Francisco Recreation and Parks
(415) 666-7079
http://parks.sfgov.org

Since the 1950s kids ages 9 months to 5 years have been gathering at rec centers, pools, and parks all over the city in organized droves of play for about half the cost of privately organized play groups. Instructors rely on parent attendance and support, and in turn they try to provide kids with an array of age-appropriate learning and fun activities that build self-esteem and social skills. Download this season's PDF from the website and find a session that's right for your child and your schedule. Cost is $4 a session, or 10 sessions for $30.

SHOPPING:
BARGAINS FOR THE
CHIC CHEAP ELITE

*"Whoever said money can't buy happiness
simply didn't know where to go shopping."*

—BO DEREK

Why pay more when you don't have to? San Francisco is home to trash-to-treasures gold mines for all styles and sensibilities. And what's better than a one-of-a-kind outfit with a past life? From no-longer-needed high-end digs to recycled H&M to a grandmother's dream closet of vintage finds, there's stuff for everyone just ripe for the plucking. But as the world of commerce surrounding vintage and shabby chic can attest, just because an item is old or previously owned does not mean that it will cost any less than if you bought its brand-new counterpart. In fact, Haight Street, Union Street, and the Mission especially can be guilty of charging deeply bloated prices for '80s miniskirts and Scooby-Doo lunch boxes simply because there is a captive audience to pay it. Enough is enough! "Antiques" and "collectibles" need not apply. This is not a directory of all the secondhand and consignment shops in town—it's simply a list of the best of those with their heads on straight when it comes to knowing what fashionable, low-priced goods with past lives should actually cost.

TOTALLY **FREE** STUFF

Craigslist's "Free" and "Barter" Categories
www.craigslist.org

My Honda Civic for your pick-up truck, my massage therapy for your Spanish lessons, my encyclopedias or dirt pile or moving boxes or queen-size futon totally free if you come and get it. . . . The possibilities are endless and manifold, but it all comes down to the same basic idea—getting stuff or trading stuff with members of your local community, no cash involved. If you're seeking something specific, this can be a great way to find it. Or if you have that compulsive shopping gene and you're short on cash, it's a great way to "catalog shop" without costing a dime. These lists are popular and change frequently, so keep your eyes peeled, act fast, and ye shall be rewarded.

Kiehl's
2360 Fillmore St.
(415) 359-9260
www.kiehls.com

Sure, the stores are located in ritzy shopping districts, but that just makes this freeloader's delight that much more pleasurable. Come in looking well scrubbed and they'll be happy to part with a free sample of any of their high-end body care and hygiene products. And with purchase, they'll practically give away the whole shop for free—a great way to try and not have to buy. Additional locations are at Neiman Marcus, 150 Stockton St. (415-362-3900), and at Saks Fifth Avenue, 384 Post St. (415-986-4300).

San Francisco Chronicle's Free Stuff Classified Ads
www.sfgate.com

Check the paper. Most of the free stuff is crap, but people have been known to dispose of their upright pianos this way.

San Francisco Freecycle Network
www.freecycle.org

Join this local chapter of the international phenomenon and let your in-box receive the bulk and bounty that the Bay Area has to offer. People pony up all kinds of one-man's-trash-another-man's-treasure goods and services that are ripe for the picking, free of charge, and simply available to any who come forward to claim them. Of course, you can also get rid of unwanted items in this forum as well. If you've got a whole apartment or clubhouse to furnish, or you're seeking a way to outfit your Burning Man camp on the super-duper cheap, this is an invaluable resource.

San Francisco Really Really Free Market
Dolores Park (18th and Dolores Streets)
www.sf-rrfm.org
Last Sat of the month, noon to 4 p.m.

It's all free. Every damn thing, and that selection varies based on who showed up and what they brought. Essentially, this is the equivalent of finding someone's discarded goods in the street, but it's conveniently located all in one place, next to a whole bunch of other stuff that no one else wants. You can get lucky, and you're likely to score if you're looking for clothes, books, foodstuffs, or what have you. This event also packs a political punch, with an anticapitalist slant in favor of the "gift economy." Feel free to donate what's been cluttering your closets.

THRIFT STORES

Community Thrift Store
623 Valencia St.
(415) 861-4910

The Catch: Service can be a little slack, but at these prices, who cares?

This is an awesome place for shopping and donating; those dropping off a carload have their choice of dozens of different charities for their belongings to benefit. There's an excellent selection of Christmas holiday goods available year-round (should you need them) plus a frequently refreshed pile of good, stylish vintage clothes; cheap books; records; and great furniture. It's all at excellent prices, particularly for the neighborhood.

Goodwill Industries

Multiple locations
1580 Mission St. (flagship store)
(415) 575-2240
www.sfgoodwill.org

The local locations of the nationwide chain are a great place to pick up work clothes for that temp job in corporate America or whenever you need cast-off department store "normal" clothes at bottom-barrel prices. Knickknacks can be hit or miss. Check out their website for area location information.

Oakland Museum White Elephant Sale

333 Lancaster St., Oakland
(510) 536-6800
www.museumca.org/events/elephant.html

This monstrous, annual springtime fund-raiser for the Oakland Museum has been happening for almost 50 years for good reason: It is a mind-blowing, department-store selection of everything in a warehouse measuring almost 100,000 square feet. While prices aren't as cheap as they could be (hey, this is a fund-raiser, after all), they're still pretty good, particularly if you're patient and willing to sort through a whole lot of trash to find that treasure. Clothes, furniture, sporting equipment, collectibles, books, music, and so very much more make it worthy of marking your calendar up to a year in advance. Check the website to see when the next event will be.

Out of the Closet Thrift Store

100 Church St.
(415) 252-1101

Founded to alchemize urban trash into funding for the AIDS Healthcare Foundation, this chain is a great overall spot for used clothes and kitchen goods. Your proceeds go to finding a cure, and three locations also offer private, on-site HIV testing and counseling. They have a somewhat better selection of used men's clothes than your average Goodwill, and your cash goes to a good cause grounded in the history and struggles of San Francisco (and beyond). Other SF locations: 1295 Folsom St. (415-558-7176) and 1498 Polk St. (415-771-1503).

Salvation Army Thrift Store

1501 Valencia St.
(415) 401-0337

If you're up for digging through monstrous piles of crap to find those one-of-a-kind goods, then this is your spot—particularly at the behemoth Valencia location. Furniture and kitchen goods, books and bags, shoes and wall hangings, and, of course, clothes to dress a small nation. Prices in the "better goods" section of the store near the front can sometimes be negotiated with manager approval. Either way, this is a giant thrifting opportunity, and bargains abound for the shrewd eyed and intrepid. Also check out the Sutter Street location: 1185 Sutter St. (415-771-3818).

Seconds to Go

2252 Fillmore St.
(415) 563-7806

While not exactly drop-dead cheap, this well-stocked clothes closet on the posh part of Fillmore carries an impressive selection of designer clothes—among them Anne Klein and Prada for men and women—at a fraction of what you'd pay for the same new. Still, it might be $40 garments rather than $400, but a bargain is in the eye of the beholder.

Worth the Trip

About an hour and a half north of San Francisco, the **Salvation Army Processing Facility and Rehab Center** in Healdsburg (200 Lytton Springs Rd.; 707-433-3334) is a Disneyland of household goods. You need a new fan? Check out the massive tables filled with hundreds of models. Looking for a new coffeepot or waffle iron? You'll have an entire room to choose from. Toys, household goods, etc., are widely available and ready to move—the only thing that's a little thin is the clothing room, which is just average, but can still unleash some pretty good finds. A snack bar is on premises to fuel your shopping pleasure.

Segunda Vuelta

1328 Valencia St.
(415) 285-9652
Mon through Wed, 10 a.m. to 3 p.m.

The Catch: The limited opening hours make it difficult to catch this tiny store open, but it's certainly worth the effort.

This tiny, eclectic secondhand shop benefits the glassy, supermodern Bethel Christian Church across the street. Despite SF's insane real estate and rental prices, here prices are kept Midwestern low: clothes for $3, knickknacks for as little as a quarter. All of this, of course, is a magnified bargain when compared to Valencia Street's otherwise tony "vintage" boutiques. Hit or miss, it's certainly worth a peek.

St. Francis's Churchmouse Thrift Shop

2408 Ocean Ave.
(415) 587-1082
Wed through Sat, noon to 4 p.m.

The Catch: Hours are limited.

When you can find it open, this is a great place for some unexpected, dirt-cheap finds. It's what thrift store shopping should be—tiny, volunteer-run, eclectic, and did I mention cheap? It was hard to find anything over $10, and considering the space, there's a good selection of women's and men's clothing, kids' clothes, toys, books, and the usual bric-a-brac.

FLEA **MARKETS**

Alameda Flea Market

2900 Navy Way, Alameda
www.alamedapointantiquesfair.com
First Sun of the month, year-round, 6 a.m. to 3 p.m. ($5 begins at 9 a.m.)

The Catch: Early birds arriving before 9 a.m. pay more for a first crack at the best goods.

No tightwad likes a cover charge, but trust us when we tell you that the $5 surcharge on this monthly shopping extravaganza is worth every nickel— even perhaps for the ridiculous view of the San Francisco skyline alone. With booths literally a mile long, the Alameda antiques fair carries everything under the sun, from clothes to antique furniture, plants to potato peelers, flatware to furniture, and zillions of doodads for the obsessive craftsperson, artist, or anthropologically oriented observer. Prices vary, with much of the antique stuff going for small fortunes, but with the right spirit, any Alameda goer is sure to come home with a treasure from times past worth the handful of pennies he or she paid for it.

Alemany Antiques and Collectibles Market
100 Alemany Blvd.
(415) 647-2043
Sun, 7 a.m. to 3 p.m.

On Saturday this lot under the I-280 overpass is a food and produce market. But on Sunday more than 250 vendors of things you wouldn't even think to look for—tools, serving platters, purses, toys, etc.—come out to peddle their wares at adjustable and solid prices. We've scored some serious loot here, and it's a great place to find presents for loved ones with an old-soul aesthetic and/or a sense of humor.

Berkeley Flea Market
Ashby BART station parking lot (Ashby Avenue at Martin Luther King Jr. Way), Berkeley
(510) 644-0744
Sat and Sun, 7 a.m. to 6 p.m.

This is a beaut of the area—particularly because it's so easy to get here via BART from SF. The happy browser will find both good prices and solid heft— and if you make reasonable offers, you'll garner a bit of haggling power. Regular items include good-quality handmade soap, an excellent selection of African art and clothing, midcentury furniture and furnishings, tube socks, Tibetan scarves and jewelry, and so very much more. Be sure to have lunch from the mobile van selling African food—delicious!

CHEAP **CLOTHING**

Aardvark's Odd Ark
1501 Haight St.
(415) 621-3141

Wasteland down the street doesn't hesitate to pedal some handmade frock from a bygone era for $50, but old Aardvark's keeps prices on simpler clothes, like button-downs and jeans, a bit easier to digest. There are lots of men's clothes here, a rarity in Haight Street's many better secondhand shops, and lots of great costume pieces to choose from (like house-made smoking jackets and frilly flapper panties) that won't break the bank.

Buffalo Exchange
1555 Haight St.
(415) 431-7733
www.buffaloexchange.com

This large national chain has a good selection of clothing at somewhat erratic, reasonable prices—though beware of the recent trend toward throwing new stuff onto the racks as well, as $25 for a T-shirt is no bargain. If you own more stylish, seasonal clothes than you know what to do with, you can bring in your duds for cash money or store credit. Don't expect to get rich quick, however: They only buy great stuff in good condition that's right for the weather. It's worth a shot, but chances are you'll be schlepping your extras to the thrift store either way. Additional locations are at 1210 Valencia St. (415-647-8332), and 2585 Telegraph Ave., Berkeley (510-644-9202).

Clothes Contact
473 Valencia St.
(415) 621-3212

Clothes by the pound! Here the savvy shopper in touch with the rules of gravity will succeed: All clothes are $10 a pound, which makes it a boon for buyers of T-shirts, lingerie, and light cotton fabrics, and just a pretty good deal for that hefty three-piece fake fur suit (though there is a price ceiling in place for heavy winter coats and such). Come here not just for clothes but also for reams of vintage fabric, scarves, ties, and other cool, retro items in bulk.

Clothing Swap
www.clothingswap.org

The Catch: Joining the swap is $25.

Find five friends your size, invite them and their unwanted clothes to your house, dump everything in the middle, and let everyone take home new attire, carting the rest to the Salvation Army on the way home. Or if this is just too much work for you, and you're a woman living in the Bay Area, you can join the rest of the "divas" paying $25 to attend this much larger clothing free-for-all that adds the benefits of goody bags, cocktails, and sometimes snacks and entertainment. Even if you leave with just a couple of garments, it's still a good value for your money. Plus you get the motivation of cleaning out your closet and donating to a noble cause. Log on to the website and sign up for the next event near you.

Crossroads Trading Company
1901 Fillmore St.
(415) 775-8885
www.crossroadstrading.com

This national chain has locations peppered throughout SF. The clothes run on the smaller, more female, more stylish side, with heaps of "cute" accessories. Each locale caters a bit to the neighborhood: The Market Street/Castro venue carries more men's clothes, for example, and the Fillmore spot tends to have a higher concentration of career and designer clothes. For that hip, urban look, this is a great place to revitalize a boring wardrobe and save a few clams in the process. Like its competitor cousin, Buffalo Exchange, it offers clothing sales and swap for any items that are no longer en (your) mode. Other SF locations include 1519 Haight St. (415-355-0555); 630 Irving St. (415-681-0100); and 2123 Market St. (415-552-8740).

Forever 21
1 Powell St.
(415) 984-0380
www.forever-21.com

Great Neighborhoods for the Penny-Pinching

Worth Avenue in Palm Beach and Rodeo Drive in Beverly Hills. Both signify what shopping in a neighborhood can deliver. The following are nothing like those two; they are simply cost-efficient solutions to acquiring the stuff that we require. Thus, here are some neighborhoods to peruse for cheap goods in San Francisco.

Clement Street between 2nd and 9th Avenues

Many shops featuring good pots and pans, cooking utensils, ceramic bowls and serving pieces, teapots, etc., many with a Japanese and Chinese aesthetic at excellent prices. This is a great place to buy gifts for others, such as pretty sets of ceramic tea accoutrements or lacquer bowls all boxed up and ready to give for as little as 10 bucks. You'll find cheap brooms, mops, plastic buckets, garbage cans, clothespins and laundry bags; off-brand, black-market toothpaste and dishwashing soap; and other assorted sundries needed for everyday living.

Mission Street between 20th and 26th Streets

Check carefully to make sure the quality level is adequate for the price—but at these prices, you shouldn't expect too much. There are backpacks and travel goods for vacationers and students, and this is one of the best places to pick up that Dora the Explorer or SpongeBob SquarePants backpack for the kids. Stock up on tube socks, cheap underwear for the whole family, and basic workout gear like sweatpants, hoodies, packaged T-shirts, and the like. Other items of note: a plethora of piñatas, fancy christening dresses for little girls, plastic flowers, and holiday decorations.

Chinatown: Grant Avenue between Bush and Broadway

Of course this is a great neighborhood for picking up Mao hats, silky Chinese pajamas, and bamboo plants for supercheap, but this stretch of Grant is also the place for visitors to find that perfect piece of SF memorabilia to bring home for a song. T-shirts, coffee mugs, paperweights, postcards, and the like are plentiful and bargain bin, as are cable car replicas, calendars, baseball hats, and more. While you're here, shop for cool oddities like wind-up sushi, slippers with spangles, and children's toys galore.

Housed in a classy old building at the Powell Street cable car turnaround, this dirt-cheap megastore is home to hot imitation couture that can be so cheap it's nearly disposable. Likely that you'll see someone else in the city donning your same duds, but the selection is so gargantuan and the styles so fleeting that it's worth the risk.

Goodbyes
Men's store: 3464 Sacramento St.; (415) 346-6388
Women's store: 3483 Sacramento St.; (415) 674-0151
www.goodbyessf.com

Stashed unassumingly on the edge of Pacific Heights (aka Specific Whites), this store's got all the high-end castaways from neighborhood ladies and gents with way too much money. Score new-to-you designer dresses, cashmere sweaters and hip handbags for a fraction of their original price. While it may be a splurge for a Cheap Bastard, Goodbyes definitely offers the high-class quality you rarely find anywhere else.

Held Over
1543 Haight St.
(415) 864-0818

Great used hipster clothes and costume supplies in great condition for a great price. What's not to love? While there are some higher prices, this Haight Street mainstay is a must-visit for the seasoned sort-through and thin-walleted urbanite. Clothes are sorted by decade, so shoppers can achieve the look they seek, and there are lots of men's clothes, coats and jackets, pajamas, etc., motivated to move.

H&M
150 Powell St.
(415) 986-4215

What IKEA is to furniture, H&M is to clothes, and ever since this Swedish bombshell descended upon Union Square in 2005, cheap-seeking, youth-oriented shoppers have been gobbling up these "fast fashions" for men, women, and children like a bowl of Swedish meatballs. New inventory pours in regularly, and most items in the mammoth, two-story discount department store are under $30—mere diddly for brand-spankin'-new, very "now" attire. Avoid the long lines and savage crowds on the weekends if you can.

Loehmann's
222 Sutter St.
(415) 982-3215

If you're female, skinny, and label conscious, you probably already know about this place, but just in case, we're here to share with you one of our best-kept secrets for new clothes on the cheap. What didn't move in major department stores across the country ends up here (or at any other of this national retailer's many locations), crammed onto racks sorted by designer, and surrounded by a never-ending drove of compulsive shoppers who would happily rip that Marc Jacobs skirt out of your hand. If you're looking to score below the ankles, Loehmann's Shoes is located across the street.

Mary's Exchange
1302 Castro St.
(415) 282-6955

This small, tightly packed Noe Valley storefront does a lot with a tiny amount of space. The focus tends to be on better vintage goods, some designer labels, and well-priced consignment with good turnover all around. Women's clothes only, with jewelry and other accessories.

Mission Thrift
2330 Mission St.
(415) 821-9560

Another great stop for great clothes, leaning heavily on T-shirts, tank tops, and simple, everyday clothes for the hip urban dweller. Don't bypass the dollar racks out front, as sometimes the finds are excellent. Though heavily bent toward women's fashions, with a good selection of purses, leggings, tights, and so on, it's also worth a stop for the guys.

Painted Bird
1360 Valencia St.
(415) 401-7027
www.paintedbird.org

OK, so it's not supercheap, but given the quality and the fact that you don't have to sort through racks of rags, Painted Bird is a great spot to hit up for fly new digs that lean to the cheap side of the scale.

Thrift Town
2101 Mission St.
(415) 861-1132
www.thrifttown.com

Make no mistake: It's got the name "thrift" in the title, but this is a for-profit enterprise. Despite this status, this locale of the national chain still boasts pretty good prices on great clothes for men, women, and kids; fantastic household items like towels, dishtowels, and bedding; and a whole floor of furniture upstairs that ranges broadly in quality but can be the site of some great archeological finds. Often offering color-tag sale specials, the place is huge and has a high turnover—you'll usually walk out with something. The tiny neighborhood newspaper, *Mission Dispatch*, frequently runs a coupon advertisement for $3 off any Thrift Town purchase of $10 or more. For your cheapskate convenience, copies of the newspaper can often be found on a newsstand at the front of the store near the check-out line.

DISCOUNT **BOOKSTORES**

Adobe Book Shop
3166 16th St.
(415) 864-3936

Adobe is a quiet, spacious shop with a great selection of both new and used. Beautiful collections of art and coffee-table books will keep you flipping. Staff is known to be generous and helpful with that in-depth literary knowledge only true San Fran bookworms possess. The discount racks out front will keep you busy while you wait for that unreliable 22 bus.

Anarchist Bookfair
http://sfbookfair.wordpress.com

Lovingly brought to you each year by the Bound Together Anarchist Collective in the Haight (where else?), this event offers low-priced books, zines, pamphlets, art, and information. Admission is always free, and browsing costs nothing. Should you choose to purchase a few tomes, prices are kept low enough so that all workers can afford them. In addition to books, there's a host of free presentations and panels for the like-minded thousands of attendees.

Bibliohead Bookstore
334 Gough St.
(415) 621-6772
www.bibliohead.com

Nestled in the midst of Hayes Valley's overpriced shoe stores and trendy bars is this used-book gem. Bibliohead is the best of the San Francisco independent bookstore scene on a small scale; you can walk in for a quick browse and find something great without getting lost in the shelves for hours. They specialize in music, dance, and opera, but they certainly have a little bit of everything, including free poetry readings the third Thursday of the month.

Black Oak Books
2618 San Pablo Ave., Berkeley
(510) 486-0698
www.blackoakbooks.com

After a few ups and downs, this Bay Area staple has found its new home. They claim their shelves are as full as ever, which means you'll find new, used, and antiquarian books, all in excellent condition, and all at good prices. Aching to clear your own shelves? Black Oak gives great offers for your gently used items every Tues and Thurs from 2 to 6 p.m. If you're looking for something in particular, check out their exhaustive online inventory before burning gas getting to the store.

Book Zoo
14 Glen Ave., Oakland
(510) 654-2665
www.bookzoo.net

Small, quaint, comfy, friendly, and well-stocked—the best of everything you expect in your independent bookstore fantasy. Old, new, and everything in between, all at fair prices. Best of all, unlike so many indie bookstore colleagues, the staff at Book Zoo is truly warm, helpful, and interested in its customers!

Dog Eared Books
900 Valencia St.
(415) 282-1901
www.dogearedbooks.com

The store is good sized but not mammoth, and yet the selection is so well honed we never walk out without something. Lots of paperbacks, including general fiction, biographies, and philosophy, at excellent prices, plus a fine selection of underground comic books, magazines, and even children's books for the liberal child. Readings and beer tastings are a great way to dive into the Dog Eared scene, but if you want to stick strictly to literature be sure to check their remainders list—new books, slightly damaged or overstocked, at discounted prices. Don't miss the free book bin!

Friends of the San Francisco Public Library Readers Cafe & Bookstore
Fort Mason, Fort Mason Center, Building C, Room 165
(415) 777-1076
www.friendssfpl.org

Half a million books are donated to the public library each year, and this outpost, open to the public, sells those that don't get logged into the stacks for as little as a dollar a piece. The selection is always changing—each month features a different theme or genre, listed on the website. Magazines, music, and videos can also be found for as little as a buck per pop. Online shopping is also offered. Be sure to check the website for the one-day, 200,000-titles-strong Friends of the Library annual book sale, where everything is $1 or less. Since your book purchases were so cheap, splurge on the available Blue Bottle Coffee while diving into your first few pages.

Green Apple Books & Music
506 Clement St.
(415) 387-2272

Consistently voted best used and best independent bookstore in the Bay Area by consumers, this truly is one of the best-stocked, largest, and oldest used-book stores in the city (now with music, DVDs, and video games, too). Plan to spend the day, because there's so much to look at, but with prices at roughly half the cover price, you won't have to spend a whole lot of cash to find something new to read.

The Magazine
920 Larkin St.
(415) 441-7737
http://themagazinesf.com

Though this shop mainly specializes in highly collectible magazines pre-1960, the 35-cent table of more recent used periodicals fills a niche like no other, particularly if you can't steal that issue of *The New Yorker* or *Food & Wine* from your doctor's waiting room. Besides a startling collection of mainstream periodicals past and present, the Magazine offers an impressive collection of old-school porn and erotica. Come to browse, to step into a time warp, or just to find something to read at a fraction of the newsstand cover price.

Modern Times Bookstore
2919 24th St.
(415) 282-9246
www.mtbs.com

This collectively owned and operated stronghold has been in motion since 1971. You won't find Ann Coulter's latest for sale here; Modern Times is progressive, lefty, political, and proud of it. In addition to a great selection of used books (political and otherwise), they also host Spanish-language book groups, queer open mics, and poetry reading events. A yearly membership will earn you a 10 percent discount on all purchases.

Moe's Books
2476 Telegraph Ave., Berkeley
(510) 849-2087
www.moesbooks.com

Moe's is a beatnik-era East Bay institution that has managed to maintain its old-school charm while keeping up on the latest literary, cultural, and political trends of the Bay. Instead of midnight openings for the newest Harry Potter, at Moe's you'll find midnight crowds lining up for the latest Pynchon release. They claim to add hundreds of used and rare titles to their collection on a daily basis, making Moe's a worthy (weekly!) destination. Check the website for changing promotions and free reading events.

Needles and Pens
3253 16th Street
(415) 255-1534
www.needles-pens.com

Cheap stuff to read doesn't just come in hardback from major publishing houses, ya know. For a dollar or two, you can widen your brain with do-it-yourself zines galore, small labors of pulp-reading love produced all over the country. They carry an excellent selection of them here, among other small-batch arts-and-crafts goods and community events, almost all of which are kept entirely affordable.

Pegasus Bookstore
2349 Shattuck Ave, Berkeley
(510) 649-1320

Repeatedly voted the best in the East Bay, Pegasus is teeming with the new, used, rare, affordable, and everything in between. This is the kind of bookstore you can make a day out of visiting. They also buy books that aren't too beat up and have resale appeal.

Serendipity Books

1201 University Ave., Berkeley
(510) 841-7455
www.serendipitybooks.com

Don't be deceived by the truly uninspiring website or the lackluster attempt to draw you to their physical location in Berkeley ("we are usually friendly"). Despite all that, Serendipity is considered one of the gems of the Bay Area independent bookseller scene. Rare first editions and out-of-prints are very much at home at Serendipity (not all of which are amenable to the Cheap Bastard budget), and you can easily spend all day winding through floor-to-ceiling caves and mazes of books. Don't expect a shopping mall experience here; a noticeable lack of signage gives your browse a feeling of adventure (or utter aimlessness!).

RECORD **STORES**

Amoeba Music

1855 Haight St.
(415) 831-1200
www.amoeba.com

Mammoth, well-loved, and well-stocked Amoeba offers a boatload of cheese-laden vinyl on sale for a buck a piece, plus the best selection of used CDs in genres so plentiful you've probably never heard of half of them. Amoeba will also buy or trade your used tunes. This is a record store you could easily spend the day in and the kind of place that makes your out-of-town visitors wish they lived here.

Aquarius Records

1055 Valencia St.
(415) 647-2272
www.aquariusrecords.org

This Mission neighborhood mainstay boasts that it is the oldest independent record store in SF, and in a city with a music history this rich, you know Aquarius is fully stocked. Chock-full of indie, punk, metal, and reggae, there's definitely something for everyone. The staff takes their store, job, and tastes seriously; go online to find exhaustive lists of recommendations, favorites, and staff picks.

Downhome Records
10341 San Pablo Ave., El Cerrito
(510) 525-2129
www.downhomemusic.com

Brimming with CDs, LPs, 45s, DVDs, and books, this music shop is worth the BART trip for those of us not satisfied storing our music collections on collapsible hard drives. Downhome's list of specialties is long, but bluegrass, gospel, country, jazz, and blues—pretty much anything with American roots—are among their strongest collections.

Rooky Ricardo's Records
448 Haight St.
(415) 864-7526
www.rookyricardos.com

All used, all the time. There's plenty to pay top dollar for here, but fear not, there are a great deal of interesting finds in an affordable price range. With 10,000 LPs in the $5 to $10 range, and 100,000 45s for $2 a pop (or 3 for $5!), even the cheapest Cheap Bastard can spruce up their vinyl collection here. This is browsing heaven for those who like to dabble around the turntable, and the vibe is pure local, friendly, and attitude free. Can't scrounge together even a few bones for a new album? Park yourself at one of the 5 listening stations and get your fix for free.

Streetlight Records
2350 Market St.
(888) 396-2350
www.streetlightrecords.com

New, used, and barely abused audible media—such as vinyl, CDs, 45s, cassettes, and yes, even video discs—are bought and sold every day for pretty good prices going both in the door and out. This is a general-interest music seller, thus you're just as likely to find classical or bluegrass as the latest hip-hop or electronica.

CHEAP **FURNITURE** &
HOME GOODS

Bernal Heights Annual Neighborhood Garage Sale
(415) 206-2140
www.bhnc.org
Every Aug

It's worth the legwork to discover the date of this mamma of all garage sales. Roughly 150 arty, affluent, city-savvy households and families clean out their storage spaces and sell what's not needed, and this is where the bargain hunter can seek, haggle, and score. Everything you can dream of is present and accounted for, from kids' stuff and yard supplies to furniture, clothes, bongs, and bongos—it's all ripe and ready to move. Get there early, and bring cash.

Center for Creative Reuse
4695 Telegraph Ave., Oakland
(510) 547-6470
www.creativereuse.org

A teacher's trove, a crafter's cash, and a Halloween costume's heaven, the Center for Creative Reuse has got it all—and more. Here you'll find everything from furniture to colored feathers, and you'll leave feeling good that you're contributing to the Bay Area movement toward the environmental-friendly economy of reuse.

Community Thrift Store
623 Valencia St.
(415) 861-4910
www.communitythriftsf.org

This massive warehouse may have every last thing you need to set up house and home on a tight budget—that is, if you're willing to dig around, look closely, and be patient. Admittedly, Community Thrift has a lot of crap that you don't want or need. They do, however, keep a decent collection of supercheap desks, dressers, comfy chairs, and couches. These pieces will probably get you the most bang for your buck, but you can easily go home with an entire set of dishware, appliances you may or may not ever use, and a shiny, black Walkman just 'cuz it made you nostalgic for the early '90s.

Cookin'
339 Divisadero St.
(415) 861-1854

Stuffed to the brims with the every kitchen need, this Divisadero diamond in the rough is a great spot for gifts and obscure culinary tools your cookbooks convince you are must-haves. From antiques to rusty "do the trick" goods, this place is perfect for both the true-blue and wannabe gourmand.

Crate & Barrel Outlet
1785 4th St., Berkeley
(510) 528-5500

All the goodies that stock the shelves of this nationwide, giant home retailer—wine glasses, place mats, couches, chairs, pillows, rugs, and so on—show up here once deemed overstocked, discontinued, or damaged. Prices are slashed anywhere from 10 to 80 percent. True bargains for better-quality stuff can be had by the frequent and patient shopper.

Dirt Cheap Mattresses
(510) 432-0500
www.dirtcheapmattress.com

The Catch: No warehouse; mattresses are shown by appointment. Cash only.

Drop a grand on a new mattress? Risk bedbugs and weirdly colored spots from someone who "sounds normal" on Craigslist? Drag that mattress in off the curb and hope for the best? The eternal mattress struggle solved at last. Dirt Cheap sells hotel-grade mattresses (new, not used, no bedbugs, stains, or questionable histories!) at 75 percent discounts. They may not be as plush or luxurious as that department store brand, but these are probably the cheapest new mattresses you'll find.

EQ3 Modern Home Furnishings
540 9th St.
(415) 552-2626

Slushing down from the Great White North, this Canadian chain of low-priced, varying quality, stylish furniture for every room of the urban hipster home is a great place to find a couch when your friend flakes on a ride to the blue-and-yellow master of Emeryville. Desks, storage, tables, beds, chairs, and household accessories abound at eye-pleasing, relatively affordable prices.

IKEA
4400 Shellmound St., Emeryville
(510) 420-4532
www.ikea.com

You hate it. You love it. You've seen the film *Fight Club* and desperately hoped that your own living room doesn't look quite so "IKEA catalog." But it's hard to resist the lure of this Swedish household retailer, which is a massive, reliable source of attractive, dirt-cheap, build-it-your-damn-self furniture for every room of the house with varying levels of quality. Don't forget that they can be cheaper than a thrift store for items like cups and plates, desk lamps, and candles, all chock-full of urban sensibility and good taste. Avoid IKEA on the weekends if you can, as the swarm of nesting couples from all over the Bay Area can be too much to endure.

Mickey's Monkey
214 Pierce St.
(415) 864-0693

We can't imagine how they can continue to pay the rent with prices so low, but this Lower Haight longtime resident is a must-visit if you're looking for a new dresser for under $100, plus a whole bunch of other well-maintained, kooky, retro household bric-a-brac, jewelry, bar sets, cool lighting, or whatever else tickles the Monkey's fancy this week. Better than junk, but still priced accordingly, their space limitations spill out onto the sidewalk and make it worth a visit.

Moving Sale
952 Howard St.
(415) 543-6833
www.movingsale.biz

Simply put, this place is a garage sale that found a more permanent home. Items are stacked floor to ceiling, and there's no guaranteeing they'll have what you need. It's worth the trip though, as prices are dirt cheap, and the sheer quantity is bound to turn up something that will tickle your fancy. Not so sure? Check out the virtual tour of the store online to see what you're getting yourself into before you go.

San Francisco Public Utilities Commission
Water Conservation
(415) 551-4730
www.sfwater.org

The PUC really, really wants you to start saving water, and to motivate you (and your landlord) to do so, they've come up with a number of cash-incentive programs to get you to go with the low-flow. For starters, they will come to your home (for free) and assess your faucets and appliances and make suggestions on how you can do your environmental part. Then you can get subsidized household plumbing and appliances. And they offer rebates: up to $125 on ultralow-flow toilets or up to $150 on the purchase of a new, green washing machine.

Urban Ore
900 Murray St., Berkeley
(510) 841-7283
www.urbanore.com

So it's not free and it doesn't benefit charity, but Urban Ore has a devotional commitment to ending urban waste by turning junk into affordable, new-to-you treasure. And indeed, Urban Ore is the place to go for any of your household or crafty DIY needs. With racks of old doors, piles of previously owned windows, drawer pulls, lamp shades, and electronic wires to suit your every need, Urban Ore offers cheap fix-it and fix-it-up solutions for the thrifty homemaker. They've also got a decent book collection, good kitchen items, and a couple clothing racks with sporadic gems. Plus you can bring along any of the things you've no longer got a use for with confidence that Urban Ore will find it all a happy home. Definitely worth the periodic trip.

HEALTH & MEDICINE:
AN APPLE A DAY

*"My doctor gave me six months to live,
but when I couldn't pay the bill,
he gave me six months more."*

—WALTER MATTHAU

Insurance? Are you kidding? At those prices? Even if you have the cheap plan, can you actually rely on it? Unless their employer is paying for health insurance, many city dwellers can't shell out the thousand smackers a month that it would cost to be protected—particularly when they're mostly healthy as an ox anyway. If you're among those without a health safety net, fear not, as there are many preventive services for physical and mental health to call upon before you head to the emergency room. Exercise, eat well, and take advantage of these sliding-scale or no-cost health-care opportunities. Most are open to everyone and don't have very-low-income restrictions, and using them doesn't take away services from the homeless or those truly in need.

MAJOR **MEDICAL**

Haight-Ashbury Free Medical Clinic
558 Clayton St.
(415) 487-5632
www.hafci.org

The name says it all. Serving more than 65,000 patients a year, this massive, long-standing sliding-scale health-care center strongly believes that medical attention is "a right, not a privilege." The clinic provides general health-care exams and advice, substance abuse programs, mental health services, and referrals to other beneficial programs.

Huckleberry Youth Services at Cole Street Clinic (HYSCS)
555 Cole St.
(415) 751-8181
www.huckleberryyouth.org

This clinic is a project of the University of California, the San Francisco Department of Public Health, and the Huckleberry House, a teen services organization. Serving clients ages 16 to 24, the clinic offers numerous types of physical care plus no-fee individual counseling, psychotherapy, and case management to teenage youth. Age-appropriate programs include birth control, HIV prevention, peer counseling, violence prevention, sensitive services, and plain-old primary care. Drop-in hours are Thurs from 2 to 6 p.m.

Lyon-Martin Health Services
1748 Market St., Suite 201
(415) 565-7667
www.lyon-martin.org

Since 1979 this not-for-profit clinic has reached out to female, lesbian, and transgender populations with quality low-cost or no-cost health-care options, now serving 2,500 patients. Tackling a major fiscal crisis in 2011, the massive burst of community support (enough, over the course of a few months, to keep the clinic alive) is testament to the quality of this clinic and its devoted staff. In addition to general health care, they cater to gynecological and hormone therapy, some fertility care, and vaccinations, immunizations, and other preventive care in English and Spanish.

Magnet
4122 18th St.
(415) 581-1600
www.magnetsf.org

Free sexual services for gay men, including sexually transmitted disease (STD) and HIV testing, as well as counseling services, hypnotherapy, and free Internet access in a stylish, intimate Castro setting. In addition, Magnet strives to be a community hub, hosting numerous events and mixers for new men in town.

North East Medical Services (NEMS)
1520 Stockton St. (main location)
(415) 391-9686
www.nems.org

Quality health care is provided in English and in a number of Asian dialects and languages, regardless of the patient's ability to pay. A staff of more than 20 physicians offers a wide range of services at 3 locations citywide, including pediatrics, dental, optometry, podiatry, cardiology, and numerous aspects of curative and preventive health. Certainly it's not fancy, but the staff is thorough, accurate, and willing to work with anyone who is considered low income or uninsured.

Planned Parenthood Shasta Pacific

(800) 967-7526
www.plannedparenthood.org/shasta-pacific/

With 30 sites across 17 Northern California counties, these clinics are still among the most reliable places for birth control and all aspects of reproductive health services at sliding-scale rates. This national organization allows local residents to calculate the cost of their appointment on the website above, based on insurance coverage (or not), income, and services sought. A good amount of informative articles and other health information is available online.

San Francisco City Clinic

356 7th St.
(415) 487-5500
www.sfcityclinic.org

Since 1911, drop-in free and low-cost reproductive health services are offered to all patients, including info on STDs, condom use, lifestyle choices, and much more. This community project features a good amount of health information on its website for men and women of all ages. Free condoms, free emergency contraception, and free post-exposure prevention are available here. The clinic has drop-in hours every day (check the website for specifics as hours vary).

San Francisco Free Clinic

4900 California St.
(415) 750-9894
www.sffc.org

The Catch: Patients cannot have medical insurance of any kind, and appointments for all services are required.

No-fee medical services, including visits with specialists, are made possible by a busy team of 160 health-care providers who donate their time, medications, equipment, and funds. With 70,000 visits under their belts, this is a great place to see an experienced provider about diabetes, vaccinations, preventative medicine—even yoga. Visits are free, but donations are accepted.

Health Insurance on the Cheap!

Healthy San Francisco, www.healthysanfrancisco.org. The perks of living in San Francisco come in all shapes and sizes, but it's hard to argue that sliding-scale health insurance is anything but the most practical and generous of perks. Healthy San Francisco is available to any adult who can prove San Francisco residency and provide basic documentation about income (you qualify if you make up to $54,000 per year). You simply choose a "medical home"—one of the city's free clinics to use as your primary-care location, and you're good to go.

Your monthly premium is based on your salary, but those in the highest income bracket will pay $50 per month tops—you won't find those prices at your local Anthem office! The best part? Even at these rates, the services covered by HSF are nothing to scoff at, especially compared to comparable city-run health coverage programs throughout the country. Emergency, urgent care, preventative, mental health, family planning, and prescriptions are all covered. The catch? You'll have to save up for vision, dental, and a number of other services—the mayor won't foot the bill for these.

Family Pact, www.familypact.org. This statewide, publically funded program provides free family-planning coverage to men and women who qualify. Birth control, education, and preventative reproductive health care are available through Family Pact for any California resident not eligible for other types of insurance or whose insurance doesn't specifically cover family planning.

San Francisco General Hospital
1001 Potrero Ave.
(415) 206-8000

A project of the city and county of San Francisco and UCSF Medical Center, this full-service, acute-care hospital refuses no one, regardless of insurance or financial ability to pay. Payment is assessed by income. It is the only facility in SF to offer 24-hour emergency psychiatric services. It also features a trauma center; children's, family, and women's health-care clinics; and general medical care.

Sister Mary Philippa Health Center
2235 Hayes St., 5th floor
(415) 750-5500

This free clinic of St. Mary's offers hands-on medical care to thousands of patients each year, either free or at a reduced rate. An advice nurse is available for free phone consultations 24 hours a day.

St. Mary's Medical Center
450 Stanyan St.
(415) 668-1000
www.stmarysmedicalcenter.org

This private Catholic hospital offers an impressive host of community outreach programs and health advice programs—simply click on the current website listings of classes and events. Lectures and roundtable discussions cover everything from health insurance counseling to living with diabetes. Community programs include free blood pressure screening and a mall walking program. Or check out the half-dozen support groups for bereavement, menopause, and more.

The Women's Community Clinic
1833 Fillmore St., 3rd floor
(415) 379-7800
www.womenscommunityclinic.org

Free, respectful, quality health care is their guarantee for their women patients, as administered by the all-women staff. General women's health, gynecological exams, and screening for STDs are the bulk of their repertoire, along with pregnancy testing and community outreach. Services are offered for all women age 12 and above.

ALTERNATIVE **HEALTH** SERVICES

The Clinic of the American College of Traditional Chinese Medicine
450 Connecticut St.
(415) 282-9603
www.actcm.org

The primary goal of this learning institution is to treat the community to the best of its ability, and it claims to be able to assist with maladies including addiction, pain, emotional well-being, and respiratory and digestive health and maintenance. They offer special rates to seniors and students and a sliding scale for the income qualified. Modalities covered include moxibustion, shiatsu, tui na, cupping, nutritional counseling, acupuncture, herbs, and more.

Depression and Bipolar Support Alliance of San Francisco
(415) 995-4792
www.dbsasf.org

Young adults, friends, and families of the DBSA are welcome to attend peer support meetings at no charge. A $20 annual membership fee is requested, but no one will be turned away. Check the website for the current schedule and meeting location.

Intercounty Alliance of Alcoholics Anonymous Serving San Francisco and Marin Counties
www.aasf.org

Those wrestling with alcohol addiction can find resources here to help them stay clean and sober, including meeting schedules, contact information, and more.

Overeaters Anonymous of San Francisco
www.oasf.org

This self-help nationwide program's local chapter keeps an updated list of meeting information, tools to jump-start an overeater's recovery, some local contact info, and more.

Quan Yin Healing Arts Center

965 Mission St., Suite 405
(415) 861-4964
www.quanyinhealingarts.com

A discount scale is offered for the uninsured, but a number of private insurances, including workers' comp, are accepted. Here patients, many of whom are chronically ill (though all are welcome), can come for treatment for whatever ails them through the channels of traditional Chinese medicine (TCM): acupuncture, massage, herbs, qi gong, and much more. The uninsured can buy a series of 4 acupuncture sessions at a significant discount. This is a nonprofit organization. Drop in hours for acupuncture are 3:15 to 5:15 p.m. on Wed; all acupuncture treatments are accompanied by a free 10-minute massage.

Reiki Center of the East Bay

1223 61st St., Oakland
(510) 653-9884
www.reikicentereastbay.com
Second and fourth Tues of the month, 7 and 8 p.m.

The low-fee clinic is run by volunteers who have been trained and are supervised at the clinic. It is designed for people who cannot afford private sessions (usually $70) or for those who cannot come during the regular workday hours. Call and arrange these low-fee sessions far in advance, as they tend to fill up quickly. Donations accepted.

San Francisco Sex Information

(415) 989-SFSI
www.sfsi.org
Mon through Thurs, 3 to 9 p.m.; Fri, 3 to 6 p.m.; Sat, 2 to 6 p.m.

Honest, nonjudgmental, and frank information about all aspects of sex and sexuality are given out at no cost and anonymously via telephone (primarily) and e-mail. The website's excellent FAQs are likely to school any curious student of the subject. Wanna ask, but can't muster the guts to make the call? Quick, responsive help can be elicited via e-mail as well by writing to ask: us@sfsi.org.

THE GREAT OUTDOORS:
THE AIR IS STILL FREE

"I believe that thrift is essential
to well-ordered living."

—JOHN D. ROCKEFELLER

As long as your lungs can pump and the rain stays at bay, San Francisco is your playground, your treadmill, and your gym. Just by walking outside nearly any day of the year, those seeking physical fitness will be greeted by temperate weather, stunning scenery, and enough hills to give even the staunchest athlete a decent reason to get hot and bothered. Think of this chapter as your personal trainer and workout coach, ripe with location-scouting suggestions to get you moving and your blood pumping. Take advantage of all that the sporting outdoors has to offer as only the Bay Area can grow it.

OUT **FOR** A **RUN** OR **WALK**

Cox Stadium
San Francisco State University campus, 19th Avenue and Halloway

The Catch: Parking is widely available here, but you'll have to pay a buck an hour.

This track never closes, but your best bet is to show up any evening after 5 p.m., when all classes and sports teams have finished their practice for the day.

Kezar Stadium
Golden Gate Park (between Stanyan and Frederick Streets)

This is one of the most popular running tracks in the city. Even when it's crowded, there's still room for all, beginner and experienced runner alike.

Lake Merced Loop
Lake Merced, Skyline Boulevard, and the Great Highway

With more than 4 miles of waterfront, paved, and flat path, this is a fine spot for auto-free running, walking, dog walking, stroller pushing, etc. It's also near a giant mall, if that sort of thing is important to you.

Bernal Hill
Bernal Heights Boulevard

For residents in the Mission District or Bernal Heights, Bernal Hill is the best place to get a dose of nature without venturing far. A 1-mile loop at the top of the hill offers sweeping views of the city, and it's easy to see why this hill in the middle of the city was once a sacred place for the Native Americans that inhabited the Bay Area.

Land's End, Lincoln Park, and Ocean Beach
Along the Great Highway

Couples have their wedding photos taken in front of the Land's End Palace of the Legion of Honor for good reason: The bay views are always breathtaking. Walk along the golf courses of Lincoln Park and the magic continues; you'll pass Seal Rock, the historic Cliff House, and the ruins of the lovely Sutro Baths along the way. Then the beach goes on—Ocean Beach, that is—and even the omnipresent fog of this Richmond District favorite cannot distract from its rapture and beauty.

Lyon Street Steps
Lyon and Green Streets

When your buns need a'crunchin', this is your Stairmaster au natural. The view is truly awesome, and the splendid homes that surround these posh digs are a sight to behold. Once you've made it to the top, you won't even notice that you're panting because the cityscape will take your breath away.

Marina Green and Fort Mason
Mason Street eastward to Aquatic Park at Beach Street

Start from the northernmost tip of the city and head east from the Golden Gate Bridge to the Marina Green and Fort Mason and continue eastward past Aquatic Park to Hyde Street Pier. The views are stunning, the paved expanse ample, and the inspiration to keep moving forward is strong. You can keep moving into Fisherman's Wharf, though the foot traffic of this tourist area may slow you down.

Public Pools

Fees are $4 per swim for adults, $1 for kids age 17 and under, plus $1 more for swimming lessons. Swim tickets are sold in books of 10 for $34. Facilities include heated pools (usually 80 degrees), showers, changing areas, and lockers, although swimmers must bring their own locks. Lessons for children and adults are offered throughout the year, as well as water aerobics, water fitness, family swims, and lap swimming. Check the current schedule to see what's offered and where at http://parks.sfgov.org.

Balboa Pool, San Jose Avenue and Havelock; (415) 337-4701

Coffman Pool, Visitacion and Hahn; (415) 337-4702

Garfield Pool, 26th Street and Harrison; (415) 695-5001

Hamilton Pool, Geary Boulevard and Steiner; (415) 292-2001

Martin Luther King Jr. Pool, 3rd Avenue and Carroll; (415) 822-2807. Two pools—a children's wading pool just 1.5 feet deep and another large pool for all.

Mission Pool, 19th Street and Linda; (415) 695-5002. An outdoor pool open only in summer, usually May to October.

North Beach Pool, Lombard and Mason; (415) 391-0407. Two twin pools 90 feet long and 9 feet deep.

Rossi Pool, Arguello Boulevard and Anza; (415) 666-7014

Sava Pool, 19th Avenue and Wawona; (415) 753-7000

The Presidio and Crissy Field
www.nps.gov/prsf/index.htm

This massive old military base is a lush, undeveloped Disneyland of the outdoors, full of tree-lined trails, miles of unhurried rolling avenues, and the Golden Gate National Recreation Area. It connects with Crissy Field, a restored landscape with great bridge views, lots of cultural activities, and a great coffee shop (the Warming Hut) on premises.

GOLF

San Francisco Municipal Golf Courses

http://parks.sfgov.org

The Catch: The city does not make obtaining a valid ID card easy.

The barrier to entry for low-cost golfing on one of SF's municipal courses may actually be more challenging than the game itself. Standard golf fees can hover near the $150 mark, truly keeping the sport's reputation as the pastime of the rich and powerful firmly on course. However, discounts are offered for many of the population in the checkered pants, including Northern California residents (around $100), seniors (around $60), juniors (around $20), and with a little legwork and persistent ingenuity, there are significant discounts offered to SF residents with valid San Francisco Recreation and Parks ID cards, with rates about a third of those of the general public. To get yours, show up in person at the treasurer's office, on the first floor of city hall, room 140, between 8 a.m. and 5 p.m., Mon through Fri. Note that applicants can only apply in person, and that these cards, annoyingly, cannot be issued at any golf course. Bring your state driver's license with SF address on it and one other piece of proof of your city residency, such as a utility bill, property tax statement, bank account statement, or any other recurring bill that has been received within the past 90 days. If your license does not have your SF address on it, you'll need two pieces of proof of residency. Pay $40. The residency card will be valid for discounts for a year, and it can be renewed by mail thereafter. The golfer in you will save up to $100 for every greens fee paid throughout the year.

Once you have your valid discount card, you are free to roam the rolling green at any of the following courses.

Chuck Corica Golf Complex

1 Clubhouse Memorial Rd., Alameda

(510) 522-4321

www.golfinalameda.com

The Catch: Residents pay $23; $27 Fri through Sun. Rates drop to as low as $18 after 3 p.m. daily.

This incredibly popular conglomerate of the Earl Fry (18 holes, par 71, 6,141 yards) and Jack Clark (18 holes, par 71, 6,559 yards) Golf Courses offers challenging 18-hole championship courses as well as the MIF Albright Executive 9-hole course with a fully lit driving range. It's flat but very windy with numerous hazards. Still, there's plenty of space for big hitters to practice for distance.

Gleneagles Golf Course

2100 Sunnydale Ave. (between Brookdale and Persia Street), McLaren Park
(415) 587-2425

This expansive green is a 9-hole course tucked into the south of the city. It can be played as a serious 18-hole course, proving to be quite challenging. Admission is only $14 during the week and $17.50 Friday through Sunday.

Golden Gate Park Golf Course

47th Avenue and Fulton Street, Golden Gate Park
(415) 751-8987
www.goldengateparkgolf.com

This 9-hole "pitch and putt" is more for fun than for serious golf, but it's easy to get to and a good choice for those just looking to get their driver wet. Summer camps for junior players are available—call for this season's offerings. No reservations are accepted; it's first come, first served. Residents pay $10 during the week, and $12 Friday through Sunday.

Harding Park and Fleming Golf Courses

Skyline Boulevard and Harding Road
(415) 664-4690
www.harding-park.com

The Catch: Harding costs residents $46; $59 Fri through Sun. Fleming costs residents $20; $22 Fri through Sun.

Open to the putt since 1930, this course is surrounded by pretty Lake Merced. Its rolling hills have a certain amount of cachet, as the course is host to the annual San Francisco City Golf Championship (one of the oldest-running amateur golf events in the country) and other tournaments attracting the likes of Tiger Woods, making it the jewel in the city's crown. True, 18-hole Harding is pricey, but with your discount it's about a third less than regular fees. Nine-hole Fleming is a "pitch and putt" course, meaning it's halfway between clown's-mouth minigolf and a real course, making it a good choice for beginners.

Lincoln Park Golf Course
34th Avenue at Clement Street
(415) 221-9911
www.lincolnparkgc.com

The Catch: Residents pay $20; $24 Fri through Sun.

Stretching around Land's End along the water's edge with breathtaking views of the Golden Gate Bridge, this forested course's stunning vistas may distract your eye from the ball. This is also one of the courses used for the annual San Francisco City Golf Championships. To make reservations—for a $1 service fee—call (415) 750-GOLF.

Sharp Park Golf Course
Sharp Park Road (off I-280), Pacifica
(650) 359-3380

The Catch: Residents pay $20; $24 Fri through Sun.

Just a few minute's drive from San Francisco to the south, this lovely day outing was originally landscaped in 1931 by John McLaren, the developer of Golden Gate Park. This 6,299-yard course sits alongside the Pacific Ocean and Laguna Salada, a natural lake ringed with plenty of flora and a variety of birds. To make reservations—for a $1 service fee—call (415) 750-GOLF.

Tilden Park Golf Course
Grizzly Peak and Shasta Road, Berkeley
(510) 848-7373

The Catch: $30; $51 Fri through Sun. After 3 p.m. the fee drops to $22; after 5 p.m. it's $15.

Here, the late bird catches the worm, as rates are deeply reduced after 3 p.m., and that can mean a hole-in-one of savings, particularly in the long days of summer. This picturesque East Bay golf attraction features 18 holes within the woodsy Berkeley Hills, where you may putt among deer and other wildlife. Lessons are available at the on-site golf learning center.

SWIMMING & **WATER** SPORTS

The Dolphin Club
500 Jefferson St.
Aquatic Park
(415) 776-7372

Founded in 1877, the Dolphin Club is a classic San Francisco institution that connects swimmers brave enough to swim the chilly waters of San Francisco Bay, who come back the next day to do it again. Today, the Dolphin Club and the adjacent South End Club buildings are open to the public on alternate days from Tuesday through Sunday. For only $6.50, members can swim in the designated area of Aquatic Park in the bay under the watchful eyes of lifeguards, while also accessing the clubs' quality facilities, including showers, saunas, and weight rooms.

Cal Sailing Club of Berkeley
124 University Ave., Berkeley
www.cal-sailing.org

Check the website for the regular schedule of free open-house days, planned most frequently during summer. Members of this enthusiastic and generous sailing club volunteer their time and their boats to take landlubbers out for an enticing, membership-building traipse around the bay when the weather conditions are right (though there is no obligation to join the club). Guests should just show up anytime between 1 and 4 p.m. in warm, waterproof clothing, and children must be at least 5 years old. Bringing a change of dry clothes may be a good idea.

City Kayak
Embarcadero at Townsend, Pier 38
(415) 357-1010
www.citykayak.com
First Tues of the month

One of the best-kept secrets in water recreation, this beautiful and mildly challenging kayak tour captures the view from the other side of the ball park, the Bay Bridge, the Ferry Building, the Embarcadero, and more. And best of all, a certain number of seats for this monthly outing don't cost a thing—save for a gratuity for your tour guide. Registration for the free seats must be made in advance by signing up on the calendar section of the website. All gear, instruction, and guides are provided, but you should bring a change of clothes and shoes just in case you end up wet. This merchant asks that users just sign up and show up; please do not call the offices to inquire about this regular giveaway.

OTHER **SPORTS**

Public Tennis Courts and Lessons
(415) 831-6302
http://parks.sfgov.org

If tennis is your racquet, San Francisco boasts more than 132 free municipal tennis courts positioned near playgrounds, parks, and recreation centers, plus an additional 21 courts in Golden Gate Park that take reservations—but there is a fee involved for the privilege. Heavily trafficked Dolores Park may have you waiting forever for an open court, but in the city outskirts, such as at St. Mary's Recreation Center in Glen Park, the courts are ready for serves almost anytime. Free beginning and intermediate classes for adults and kids are offered throughout the year. Students must bring their own racket, wear good tennis shoes, and donate a can of unopened tennis balls to play and learn. No drop-ins; reservations are required. The schedule of classes can be found on the website.

The San Francisco Lawn Bowling Club
Bowling Green Drive (near Sharon Meadow and the Carousel),
Golden Gate Park
(415) 487-8787
Wed at noon; additional evenings in summer, or by appointment

The Catch: Reservations are needed for evening instruction, and flat-soled shoes are required.

One needn't be a white-clad septuagenarian to play the balls, but it would help if you want to fit in with this crowd. After watching members bowl their black orbs on the club's pristine expanse of green, bystanders have free weekly opportunities to try their own hand at the sport, with teachers who are always graciously willing to share the skills.

Skateboarding in Crocker Amazon Park
Moscow and Italy Streets
(415) 337-4708
http://parks.sfgov.org

Helmets and protective padding are excellent ideas—almost as good as letting your teenagers or older kids thrash to their heart's content.

Skateboarding at Potrero del Sol Park
25th and Utah Streets

This newly opened skate park has been a major hit with expert shredders, skating bigwigs, and novices alike. Potrero del Sol provides a free place for all to test their skills or learn the craft at one of the most culturally diverse skate parks around.

FITNESS:
WORKING IT OUT

"You can't leave footprints in the sands of time if you're sitting on your butt. And who wants to leave buttprints in the sands of time?"

—BOB MOAWAD

Let's face it: We love San Francisco's many twists and quirks, but the crummy winter weather—hell, even the crummy summer weather—can make any urbanite wonder why we left wherever it was that we migrated from. Despite the bouts of fog, cold, and rain, the body must move, but the expense of a gym membership can be so depressing that it might take a whole box of Twinkies to brighten our spirits. Fortunately, the flexible cheapskate with her ear to the ground will find that bargains, even in the realm of the indoor workout, can abound. Read on . . . and Twinkies be damned, you will learn how to tighten your wallet as well as your muscles.

FREE & **DISCOUNTED** GYMS

ABADÁ-Capoeira San Francisco Brazilian Arts Center
3221 22nd St.
(415) 206-0650
www.abada.org

The Catch: Cash or local checks only, and the $32 discounted pass must be used within 30 days.

We cannot guarantee that you'll be spinning through the air in a split in the first 30 days, but it's worth a shot, and you're promised a guaranteed-to-sweat workout in the process. Brand-new adult students can purchase a discounted pass for 4 classes for $32, a substantial savings over the $12 drop-in fee. Regular class fees are slightly lower for kids under 19 years old, and some financial assistance may be available for low-income youth.

Aikido Center
1755 Laguna St.
(415) 921-5073
www.pacific-aikido.org/sfcenter.html

Forget the one-time drop-in-and-taste approach to discipline and fitness offered by most gyms: Here beginning students have 3 weeks, at 2 sessions a week, to decide if aikido in Japantown is the right course of action to fit their lifestyle. At just $9 a session, and with the flexibility to take the beginner's course as many times as you like, this is a license to stretch your physical as well as cultural muscles.

Berkeley Ironworks
800 Potter St., Berkeley
(510) 981-9900
www.touchstoneclimbing.com

This East Bay cousin to the popular Mission climbing gym is larger and offers a greater variety of workout classes, like cardio-kickboxing, core strengthening, yoga, kids' programs, and more. They also offer the same great price break for daytime climbers—just 10 bucks before 3 p.m. on weekdays.

Curves
www.curves.com

The Catch: Free trial membership . . . and membership pitch.

At last count there were 20 locations around the bay and 10,000 worldwide. Each is a franchise, thus the rules and policies may be slightly different, depending on which location you choose. Most offer some sort of no-obligation trial, either a week's free membership or a small handful of consulting sessions with a personal trainer. As with all gyms, expect a pretty hard sell if you do indeed come in or give up your contact information. But if you're looking to get on some Nautilus machines gratis, this is your gateway.

Krav Maga
1455 Bush St.
(415) 921-0612
www.kravmaga-sf.com

The Catch: Free trial class . . . and membership pitch.

If you've ever been interested in the kind of workout that can spout from an Israeli/CIA self-defense and fighting strategy, this is your chance to try it and not lose a single shekel. Call or send your contact info via the website, along with a good time to reach you, and they will sign you up for a free trial class and a free, celebrity-studded DVD. They also offer complimentary group training sessions for your group, corporate team, or nonprofit organization, covering the basics of self-defense and a fighting spirit.

Mission Cliffs

2295 Harrison St.
(415) 550-0515
www.touchstoneclimbing.com

If getting your butt in a sling and hanging off a rock is your idea of fun, then this indoor rock-climbing extravaganza is your mountaintop just ready to be summited. Get here before 3 p.m. on weekdays and it's just $10 to drop in and climb, saving you $8 off the regular price paid by the after-work crowd. The first Friday of the month is women's night, and the third Friday night of the month is college student night. On both occasions, qualified attendees get in for just $10 (in the case of the students, valid ID is required).

24 Hour Fitness

www.24hourfitness.com

This nationwide chain has 10 San Francisco locations, and they're sweetening the trap to help bring you into its well-toned folds: Sign up for either 10 free days of gym membership or 15 free days of workout classes and gym membership. Should you decide to join, the site offers other incentive programs, such as printable coupons to help you skip the initiation fee. Of course, none of this is possible without giving up your full contact info, so proceed with caution.

FREE **OR** CHEAP **YOGA**

Yoga to the People

2973 16th St., 5th floor, San Francisco
64 Shattuck Sq., Berkeley
(917) 573-9642

The first yoga studio to run multiple studios solely on a donation basis, Yoga to the People is committed to making asana practice more accessible, which is great news for the yogi who is looking for a consistent place to practice without breaking the bank. With studios in both San Francisco and Berkeley, and a schedule that offers morning and evening classes, Yoga to the People earns extra points for accessibility and convenience. Because these classes are all "pay what you can," they fill up, fast. So be sure to arrive to the class of your choice at least 15 minutes early with your mat and towel, and pay whatever you can afford on your way out!

Bija Yoga Studio
1348 9th Ave.
(415) 661-9642
www.bijayoga.com

Compared with the usual drop-in fees, 10 bucks per class for 5 classes is a bargain that will have any aspiring yogi or yogini breathing easier.

Integral Yoga Institute
770 Dolores St.
(415) 821-1117
www.integralyogasf.org

Pictures of the resident Sri Swami Satchidananda hang on the institute's wall, yet the yoga and meditation community they're seeking to build is entirely affordable. The regular hatha class drop-in fee is just $11, and always only $8 for those over age 62, for those with HIV, and for first-time students. In addition, open meditation classes are offered daily. And on Tuesday and Friday, lunch can be had after the regular meditation session for just $5 (prearrangement required). Work trade for classes can also be arranged.

Laughing Lotus Yoga Center
3271 16th St.
(415) 355-1600

This popular yoga center started in New York and, after years of success in the Big Apple, opened a sister center in San Francisco in 2008. In addition to being one of the best yoga studios in the Bay Area, the Laughing Lotus has daily donation-based classes from 2:30 to 3:50 p.m., as well as a stellar deal for students visiting the studio for the first time: $20 for an unlimited week of yoga. If that's not enough reason to check out this studio, graduates of the excellent Laughing Lotus Teacher Training program also offer community classes at the Women's Building located at 3483 18th St. These classes run Mon and Wed evenings from 6 to 7:15 p.m., with a suggested donation of $5.

Prenatal Yoga Classes

St. Luke's Hospital
3555 Cesar Chavez St.
(415) 824-0663
Sat, 10 a.m.

Just show up—no experience or preregistration is necessary. Wear something comfortable, and let instructor Susan Arthur help moms-to-be relax and ease aching backs and hip joints in these free sessions.

Rusty Wells's Urban Flow

At ABADÁ-Capoeria San Francisco Brazilian Arts Center
3221 22nd St.
(415) 333-YOGA
www.rustywells.com

The Catch: Suggested donation is $15.

The entirely charismatic Rusty has a loyal following, so much so that this crowded room of pay-what-you-can regular devotees pays enough to keep him afloat. The suggested donation is a standard $15, but no one gives you the hairy eyeball as long as you put something in the donation box. Get there early, bring a towel and some water, and prepare to work on your body and breath. Call the phone number listed above or check the website for his ever-changing schedule. Note that Rusty teaches many classes all over town, but only those at ABADÁ are donation based.

Sivananda Yoga Vedanta Center San Francisco

1200 Arguello Blvd.
(415) 681-2731
www.sfyoga.com

The Catch: First class free; $10 thereafter, with bulk discounts available.

This global nonprofit center offers a wide variety of Eastern practices, including some ayervedic courses, vegetarian cooking, and meditation, but they're mainly known for their yoga for practitioners of all levels. Check the schedule and drop by anytime, as the first time you hit your mat is on the house! After that, regular drop-in classes are 10 bucks a pop, with bulk discounts available.

The Yoga Loft
321 Divisadero St.
(415) 626-5638
www.theloftsf.com

New students can benefit from their first 3 classes at just 10 bucks a pop (when bought all at once), but existing students also qualify for rewards, such as an $11 student price and free classes for regular passholders when you bring a friend. Check the schedule for community classes, open to all, for $10.

Yoga Tree
519 Hayes St.
(415) 626-9707
www.yogatreesf.com

With 4 locations around the city, this mini local chain offers a wide variety of classes, instructors, and styles. For the student new to the Tree, they offer a substantial discount on your first handful of classes—3 classes for $20— something to be taken advantage of when contrasted with the $16-per-class regular drop-in fee. Check the schedule for off-hour community classes, where entry for anyone and everyone is just $8. Other locations include 780 Stanyan St. (415-387-4707); 1234 Valencia St. (415-647-9707); and Yoga Flow Castro, 97 Collingwood (415-701-YOGA).

MEDITATION: **FREE** YOUR **MIND**

Brahma Kumaris Meditation Center
401 Baker St.
(415) 563-4459
www.bksanfrancisco.com

This local venue is connected to the group's 7,000 other centers in 80 countries, and as such it has the resources to offer a panoply of free classes, meditation sits, and retreats, some drop-in and some with reservations required. There's even "power" meditation and lunchtime sits in the Financial District for the busy but mindful, courses of study offered in Spanish, and courses specifically for women, men, and seniors. Check the schedule to find out what's currently on offer.

East Bay Meditation Center
2147 Broadway Ave., Oakland
(510) 268-0696
www.eastbaymeditation.org/

The East Bay Meditation Center is an oasis of peace and stillness amidst the hustle and bustle of downtown Oakland. Offering a variety of classes including People of Color meditation groups, LGBT groups, and groups open to everyone, the East Bay Meditation Center is one of the most diverse *sanghas* around. This is a wonderful place for people new to meditation as well as those who have been practicing for many years to come and look within in an environment committed to social justice and inclusion.

Insight Meditation Community of San Francisco
Starr King Room of the First Unitarian Universalist Church of San Francisco
1187 Franklin St.
(415) 994-5951
www.sfinsight.org
Sun, 7 to 9 p.m.

This long-standing and active *sangha* (Buddhist community) offers weekly sits and dharma talks, a rotating schedule of monthly events for those new to meditation practice, and a monthly potluck dinner. Tap into this community to hear about affordable (though not free) courses, workshops, and more to help deepen the practice of the serious lay student.

Mission Dharma Weekly Vipassana Meditation
St. John's Episcopal Church
1661 15th St. (entrance through the garden on Julian Street)
(415) 447-7761
Tues, 7:30 to 9 p.m.

The church is not the spiritual base but rather just a meeting place of this weekly Buddhist meditation community as led by teacher Howard Cohn. Practitioners sit for roughly 40 minutes, take a short tea break, and then stay for a 45-minute dharma talk. There is no fee to attend, but a basket sits by the door to help cover the cost of the room rental and to collect funds to cover the cost of the teaching.

San Francisco Meditation Group
385 Ashton Ave.
(415) 584-8270
www.srf-sanfrancisco.org

This meeting group of the Self-Realization Fellowship, an organization founded by Paramahansa Yogananda in the 1920s, holds weekly meditation and reading sessions that are open to the public gratis.

San Francisco Shambhala Meditation Center
1630 Taraval St.
(415) 731-4426
http://sfshambhala.org

The schedule of this mindfulness-based worldwide style of Buddhist meditation changes; it's an excellent introduction to the practice and a great foundation to shape the beginner's mind. The center offers free midweek evening introductory sessions as well as Sunday morning open houses and Saturday daylong retreats open to the public and gratis (though their hope is to have interested parties join as members of their community to keep their organization afloat).

LEARNING & LECTURES: YOU'VE GOT CLASS

"Lack of money is no obstacle.
Lack of an idea is an obstacle."

—KEN HAKUTA

One cannot put a value on the price of an education—but it's always better to learn something for free. Luckily, San Francisco is a locale dedicated to self-improvement and enrichment at every turn, and there is no shortage of low-cost and no-cost organizations and opportunities to school you for a song. From bike repair to gardening to violin lessons and to the intricacies of world politics, you and your brain have many avenues to explore that won't cost much more than the time it takes to sit and listen. Sharpen your pencils and grab a recycled notebook. We've got a lot to learn.

GENERAL **EDUCATION**

Berkeley Adult School
1701 San Pablo Ave., Berkeley
(510) 644-6130
http://bas.berkeley.net

Providing quality education since 1881, this unique public school for adults offers a host of classes to the public for free, including instruction in ESL, basic education courses, and high school diplomas. Classes for adults with disabilities and older adult classes are free. The general public is welcome to sign up for very-low-cost courses in subject areas designed to enrich the quality of life or career, including job and office skills, the arts and social sciences, theater and financial planning, and a whole lot more.

The Curiosity Guild
3824 Mission St.
(415) 839-6404

From glass etching to jam making, growing herb gardens to running an eBay business, with a few CD exchanges and gallery tours in between, members of the loosely organized, bicoastal guild teach fun and mission-critical skills to one another and the public at regular monthly intervals for a reasonable fee—usually in the neighborhood of $25 or so. Check the calendar or their blog for a list of current events.

Richmond Village Beacon, a Program of the Richmond District Neighborhood Center

George Washington High School
600 32nd Ave., T3
(415) 750-8554
www.rvbeacon.org

This bustling community center offers myriad after-school programs for middle and high school students plus an impressive array of free life-skills courses for young adults ages 18 to 25. Committed students have the opportunity to learn real hands-on job skills, cooking know-how, renter's rights, personal financial management, and much more to arm themselves with the knowledge they need to make daily life better. Those who successfully complete the courses often receive a retail cash incentive to help them put their newfound knowledge to good use, such as a gift certificate to a hardware store or an electronics store. Less utilitarian, but more fun, yoga, tai chi, knitting, and dance classes are also popular. Advanced registration is required.

San Francisco City College

50 Phelan Ave.
(415) 239-3000
www.ccsf.edu

At just $20 per credit unit for California residents, this full-service learning institution offers a wide array of classes at all hours of the day or evening for those seeking a college degree or simply their own personal fulfillment. Placement services and career counselors make it possible to learn a new career on the cheap.

Even if you're not a paying student, the school offers a full calendar through most of the year of interesting films, concerts, lectures, and more. Check the calendar to take advantage of this gold mine of free happenings.

San Francisco Public Library

Various locations
(415) 557-4400
www.sfpl.org

Though there's a heavy emphasis on the weekly roster of typing, Internet usage, and computer skills, the giving tree of your local public library offers

Stop Spinning Your Wheels—DIY Bike Repair

A chain of local enterprises will teach you the fine, free art of bicycle repair, handling, and safety.

Missing Link Bicycle Cooperative, 198 Shattuck Ave., Berkeley; (510) 843-7471; www.missinglink.org. Fix your own flat, build your own wheels, and understand the tao of brakes and gears. All classes are taught by this collective's incredibly seasoned panoply of professionals, and they're offered as a public service to anyone on two wheels.

Pedal Revolution, 3085 21st St.; (415) 641-1264. Lecture and demonstration repair clinics are offered periodically, and regular attendees can learn the skills they need to keep their steed well-tuned and operating. Call the store to find out what they're teaching next.

San Francisco Bicycle Coalition, 995 Market St., #1550; (415) 431-BIKE; www.sfbike.org. Check the calendar to find the current schedule of bicycle safety classes designed for anyone who navigates SF's mean, car-hogging streets. Learn about safety equipment, proper hand signals, and more. Preregistration is required.

the occasional crafts course, guides to unraveling the enigma of city government, and education on how to get the most out of library resource materials, to name a few. Of course, these are your tax dollars at work. Don't think of these classes as just free. Think of them as already paid for.

ARTS & SCIENCES

Ask a Scientist Night
1200 9th Ave.
(415) 504-0060
www.askascientistsf.com

The Catch: This is a free event, but it's held inside the large and bright art cafe. Prepare to pay for at least a cup of coffee if you plan to fill a seat.

Why do scientists study monkeys? What's the skinny on forensic science, the future of the electric car, and what, exactly, does $E=mc^2$ mean? Come absorb the brain dump of this very popular monthly lecture series that puts real live know-it-alls in the various fields of science in front of a leisurely, knowledge-hungry cafe crowd. Voted best place to get an expert opinion by the *San Francisco Bay Guardian,* stick around after the lecture so you can show everyone how smart you are at the lengthy Q&A session. Sign up for the mailing list as event locations vary.

CounterPULSE

1310 Mission St.
(415) 626-2060
www.counterpulse.org

The Catch: A $3 to $5 donation is requested, but no one is turned away for lack of funds.

On the second Sunday of the month this activist arts organization hosts an excellent lecture series for one and all, in the form of free salons where choreographers engage audiences to hash out their art form. Not into the dance scene? Come and learn about the city's fascinating untold liberal history, and get an insider's look at the local politics that shaped this town. These topics intermingle with subjects of an ecological nature, such as a local frog restoration project or the general greening of the city. Periodic film nights on local topics round out the repertoire. This arts organization also has an evolving calendar of very affordable classes in every aspect of performance.

Harvey Milk Photography Center

Harvey Milk Recreational Arts Building
50 Scott St.
(415) 554-9522
www.sfphotocenter.com (class schedule only)

The Catch: Membership gets you the discount.

The budding shutterbug inside you will be happy to learn about photographic composition, negative development, and the mechanics of photo printing—and to attend classes that cost a fraction of what you'd pay elsewhere. The use of the darkroom is also enlightening for your wallet—just $50 for 6 months of access. Total beginners and studio professionals are welcome, but all must attend a free midweek orientation in order to become a member.

San Francisco Art Institute
800 Chestnut St.
(415) 771-7020
www.sanfranciscoart.edu

Are there any words more sweet and ethereal than "free and open to the public"? If you, too, get a little lightheaded at the phrase, and you enjoy opening your mind to an expanding world of experienced and cutting-edge artists in multiple formats, this regular series of artist lectures will surely round out the mind. The artists who show and screen at this acclaimed school's galleries have a chance to share their vision during informal, and complimentary, evening discussions.

San Francisco Comedy College
442 Post St., 5th floor
(415) 921-2051
www.sfcomedycollege.com

The Catch: Preregistration gets you the free lesson.

Is it a free lesson or a sales pitch? You be the judge. Either way, those who preregister are permitted to attend a single, midweek evening of free lessons in what makes you, and the jokes that you tell, so darn amusing. And while your butt warms the chair, you'll learn more about classes at the college and what they can do to get you a stint on *Letterman.*

Sharon Art Studios
Golden Gate Park Children's Playground
(415) 753-7004, (415) 753-7006
www.sharonartstudio.org

The Catch: Additional material fees and studio fees may be required for some classes.

Adult and youth arts and crafts classes are offered at excellent prices, as subsidized by the San Francisco Recreation and Parks Department. For as little as $40 for an 8-week kids' course, or $85 for a 10-week adult course, students can unleash their left brain on ceramics, lead glass, metal work, enameling, drawing, watercolor, and more. Short of studying the work of graffiti artists in the streets, this is some of the most inexpensive arts education available.

Terra Mia Decorative Art Studio

1314 Castro St.
(415) 642-9911
www.terramia.net

The Catch: $10 for facilities use per day, with some special discounts available.

This underrated ceramic arts studio already has low prices—just $10 for unlimited use of the facilities for an entire day, and half price for kids. However, first-time customers who know their way around a keyboard and a pottery wheel can print out an online coupon and save a few bucks with a 20 percent off Web coupon and other specials. Returning clay slingers should check their monthly calendar for periodic free days and 2-for-1 specials.

Workshop

1798 McAllister St.
(415) 874-9186
www.workshopsf.org

The Catch: Most classes are $30 to $40, but this covers materials needed for your craft that you get to keep when you leave.

Feeling crafty, but don't know where to start? Workshop gives you a plethora of crafting options beyond your grandma's sewing kit. Classes are small, affordable, and taught by people who are surprisingly expert! Knitting and crocheting are just the beginning; Workshop offers classes in bike maintenance, brewing ginger beer, and producing your own glass jar terrariums (to name a few). It's a do-it-yourself haven in the heart of NOPA, and the best part is you never leave empty-handed. Be sure to sign up online early—the most popular classes sell out weeks in advance.

FOOD & **WINE**

Bartending School of San Francisco

760 Market St., Suite 833
(415) 362-1116
www.sfbartending.com

The first 3.5-hour class is totally free to those who register in advance, and serious students can even apply this education toward a completion certificate in bartending. Of course the school hopes that those who show up at one of these freebies will sign on to complete the course in its 10 full sessions, but there is no obligation. Students will learn the proper mixology behind 16 different elixirs. And no, drinks will not be served.

City College of San Francisco's Continuing Education Courses on Wine and Food
Fort Mason Art Campus
Laguna Street and Marina Boulevard, Building B
(415) 561-1860
www.ccsf.edu

The Catch: Classes aren't necessarily cheap, but the wine courses are a bargain.

The cooking classes here—everything from the knowledge of cupcakes to sushi making to cheese tasting and appreciation—are a bit cheaper than most other one-day courses through retail chains, usually around $50 or so for an evening, but not a mammoth bargain. The real surprise and savings from this school for the rest of us comes from the wine courses, usually costing under $100 for a 4-week session. The budding sommelier will be hard pressed to find a wine appreciation course at any comparable cost. Check this semester's course catalog for what's ripe on the vine. Sign up one week in advance to receive a sizable registration discount.

CUESA Market to Table Events
Ferry Building Farmers' Market
1 Ferry Building, Suite 50
(415) 291-3276
www.cuesa.org
Sat morning

The Center for Urban Education about Sustainable Agriculture (CUESA) serves up a delicious weekly menu of lectures, demonstrations, and informative cook-offs that showcase the best of seasonal foods and the best culinary talent of the Bay Area culinary elite. In addition to their monthly fetes like the Asparagus Festival or a celebration of mushrooms, local chefs offer cooking demos, jam making how-tos, and DIY cocktail lessons. The patient and intrepid can linger afterward for a taste of what was prepared before their eyes. Get the newsletter to be kept abreast of other periodic events, such as free author readings with a food theme, local farm tours, and more.

MEDIA

The Long Now Foundation
Fort Mason Center, Landmark Building A
(415) 561-6582
www.longnow.org

The Catch: A $10 donation is requested for each attendee, but "it is certainly not required for attendance." Also note that because the lectures are unticketed, seats tend to disappear quickly.

What Slow Food is to the culinary arts, Long Now is to philosophy and thought. Brian Eno's pet project, this organization hosts a monthly lecture series that focuses on a different meaning of "here" and "now" as they pertain to a broader, slower scope of thinking. The speakers challenge attendees to ponder their personal responsibility when they consider the world, and this popular lecture series reflects this genre of thought.

Media Alliance
1904 Franklin St., #500, Oakland
(510) 832-9000
www.media-alliance.org

The old, gray-bearded workhorse of the alternative media scene provides a slew of resources for the budding and seasoned journalist, including a job file, courses in everything from ethics to editing, and speaker events with the top names of the left-wing brigade. All of this costs money to produce, but it is also made possible by the sweat equity of its supporting community, and this could mean you. Simply work a set number of hours in exchange for partaking in what this well-versed organization has to offer. Contact them for more information.

World Affairs Council
312 Sutter St.
(415) 293-4600
www.itsyourworld.org

President Jimmy Carter, Wesley Clark, and Willie Brown have all stepped into the ring of this international organization. It hosts 200-plus events per year that invite discussion on local, national, and international politics and topics. You, too, opinionated newshound, are welcome to join their ranks at any of their regular discussion platforms, including meetings exclusively for young adults, library lectures, school and corporate programs, and more. Many gatherings are free, many more are free to members, and those that do charge an admission fee tend to be affordable, in the $5 to $15 range. With attendance, those interested in political tectonics and socioeconomic shifts cannot help but learn more about their world. Check the current calendar for what's happening this month.

SPIRITUALITY

Bureau of Jewish Education Jewish Community Library
639 14th Ave.
(415) 751-6983
www.bjesf.org/events.htm

From genealogy to Jews in the Jazz Age, a number of free talks and community events are held here in collaboration with the excellent library resources. They showcase Judaism not just from a religious perspective but from a thriving, modern, living point of view. All events welcome the general public to simply drop in and learn. The handful of events offered monthly changes often; consult the website to see what's on now. For those seeking more information on the nuts and bolts of the religion, find out when this year's Feast of Jewish Learning takes place. This is an outreach program for anyone wishing to learn more about Jewish education and practice.

Psychic Horizons

970 Valencia St.
(415) 643-8800
www.psychichorizons.com

In the tradition of mediation and self-help workshops, this school and psychic reading center has been in the neighborhood for 20 years, and it continues to attract an interested (and interesting!) crowd. On Mon night come ready with a single question for a free reading, Tues at 7:30 p.m. a free intro to meditation classes is offered, and free weekend clinics offer readings and healing sessions as a way for students to practice the craft they study. There are also coupons galore on the website for healing and clinics to be scheduled at any time.

Yoga Society of San Francisco

2872 Folsom St.
(415) 285-5537
www.yssf.com

Those with more spirit than disposable income will find a host of free holistic opportunities, such as complimentary daily fire ceremonies, mantra classes, and meditations. Check the calendar for regular monthly work days (when volunteers are given a vegetarian lunch in exchange for their good karma) and also periodic "yoga days," featuring an entire day of free instruction at no cost (though donations are welcomed).

TECHNOLOGY & **BUSINESS**

Computer Workshops at the Apple Store

1 Stockton St.
(415) 392-0202
www.apple.com/retail/sanfrancisco

Mac users, rejoice! The Union Square flagship store features a full calendar of nearly a dozen daily courses designed to broaden and sharpen your Mac user skills. From pros to beginners, there are educational opportunities designed for all, at no cost, with no obligation to buy a thing. It's first come, first served (and seats can go quickly, especially on the weekend) for classes in GarageBand, podcasting, high-definition filmmaking, wireless networking, and much more. Drop in and make retail sing for its supper.

Foundation Center
312 Sutter St., Suite 606
(415) 397-0902
http://foundationcenter.org/sanfrancisco

Though primarily geared toward serving the grant-seeking needs of the non-profit sector, individual grant seekers can take advantage of this esteemed organization's generous resources to help draw attention and cash money to your personal philanthropic venture. Register for one of the free, regular courses in how to find funding, how to write a grant proposal, and how to target organizations that are most likely to fund your project. Learn how to use the excellent library of resources, a valued tool in the philanthropic community for 50 years.

San Francisco Women on the Web
www.sfwow.org

This networking organization offers great grassroots networking (1,300 members strong!) via the popular Scrappy Hour—a male and female mixer for anyone interested in meeting more people in the technology industry, where the only thing you need to pay for are the business cards in your pocket and the drink in your hand. Women in the field will want to take advantage of the popular and chatty mailing list, the intimate (and free) Coffee Klatch roundtables, and the low-cost classes in programming.

Small Business Administration of San Francisco
455 Market St., Suite 600
(415) 744-6820
www.sba.gov/ca/sf

From basic bookkeeping to accepting credit cards for your online business, the classes at this government-sponsored organization's local leg teach real and helpful skills for the enterprising individual—free or at subsidized fees. There are even classes in effective time management, and who couldn't benefit from that? The monthly, 1-, and 2-session classes change often. See what's on schedule to help your business, or your business idea, grow. Note that courses are taught in English and Spanish.

HEALTH & **WELLNESS**

Bay Area Wilderness Training
2301 Broadway, Suite B, Oakland
(510) 452-BAWT
www.bawt.org/train/skill_builders.php4

While this organization's main goal is wilderness leadership training for youth, it offers several community programs a month to boost the knowledge of any backwoods backpacker. Build your skills in the great outdoors by taking advantage of the free course offerings about aspects of first aid, including bandaging and splintering, and patient assessment. Graduates of their training courses are allowed to borrow BAWT's wilderness camping gear for free. Details are available on the website.

Integrative Medicine Today at the Osher Center
1545 Divisadero at Post Street, 5th floor
(415) 353-7700
www.osher.ucsf.edu/public/lunchtime.html
Second Thurs of the month, noon to 1 p.m.

Anyone seeking to broaden his or her knowledge of mental affirmations in health care and alternative modalities is welcome to attend these free informal and informative lectures hosted by the University of California's School of Medicine. Massage, Chinese medicine, meditation, and a slew of alternative therapies for chronic disease are discussed, including their positive effects when used in collaboration with traditional Western medical practices. Attendees are asked to bring their own brown bag lunch and eat while they learn. No preregistration is required.

Neighborhood Emergency Response Team Training
Sponsored by the San Francisco Fire Department
(415) 970-2022
www.sf-fire.org

After the 7.1 earthquake that shook the city in 1989, this intensive, free course in how to survive and sustain the next natural disaster set out to educate the public with widespread success. Today, all are welcome to sign

Green Energy

We need not burn through the environment. If you want to be more conscientious but aren't sure how to do it, these resources will show you that it's easy to be green.

Building Resources, 701 Amador St.; (415) 285-7814; www.building resources.org. Artists and contractors alike will revel in this incredible hands-on resource in green building and clean living through recycled materials. The free course offerings at various Bay Area locations are a tremendous resource, and for just a few dollars in materials fees, they will teach you the likes of lamp building, environmental education and landscaping, and more. Once you have the know-how to use their vast inventory of recycled materials, they will provide you with the goods to launch your new project, including plywood, tile, wood, and bricks on sale at reasonable, community prices.

PG&E Classes in Energy Efficiency, 851 Howard St.; (415) 973-2277; www.pge.com. Pacific Gas & Electric sells the power, yet ironically it's willing to provide the general public with information to help people use less. In addition to its free classes for contractors and building professionals, PG&E offers up the latest thinking on topics like solar power, green building, and photovoltaic systems design. Registration is required, and classes seem to fill up fast. If the SF courses are packed, students can try to enroll in courses in Oakland, San Jose, Concord, and elsewhere—including online.

up and learn how to help themselves and their community when disaster hits the fan next time around. At prominent locations all over San Francisco, residents are just 6 sessions away from being a local hero and learning critical skills like how to wield a fire extinguisher, how to shut off the gas, search and rescue techniques, how to pack a survival kit, and much more.

GARDENING

Garden for the Environment
451 Hayes St., 2nd floor
(415) 731-5627
www.gardenfortheenvironment.org

The Catch: Preregistration is required for the popular and celebrated courses, and some materials fees may apply.

Dying to get your urban beekeeping on? Baffled by compost conundrums? Free and very-low-cost courses will teach you how to grow edible and environmentally harmonious plants and learn the basics of everything from nurturing fruit trees to winter pruning to using recycled materials in your home garden. Several classes are offered every month, and no one will be turned away for lack of funds.

Hayes Valley Farm
450 Laguna St.
www.hayesvalleyfarm.com

This downright magical spot in the middle of the city is a true community masterpiece. Transforming the site of the pre-earthquake freeway ramp into a lush, bustling community garden is no small feat, but that's exactly what this group has done, and they're happy to share the fruits of their labor and their wealth of gardening knowledge. Volunteer days are Sunday and Thursday, where you can chip in building plant beds, planting, and composting.

San Francisco Garden Resource Organization (SFGRO)
P.O. Box 170396, San Francisco CA 94117
(415) 235-4292
www.sfgro.org

Free composting workshops and more are offered by this nonprofit, green-thumbed organization.

LIBRARIES:
FREE ACCESS

"Money is of no value; it cannot spend itself.
All depends on the skill of the spender."

—RALPH WALDO EMERSON

Last we checked, reading and listening are still free, and San Francisco's overeducated community offers about a zillion resources to help you master the intricacies of the world around you, whether it is local art happenings, politics, health care, or the beauty of the esoteric and obscure. Choose your method—print, airwave, etc.—and soak it all in. Anyone with an attention span can stay informed, educated, and independent of the corporate media giants that have come to dominate the industry. Here are a few of SF's best free "classrooms" to get you started.

Barnett-Briggs Medical Library
San Francisco General Hospital Medical Center
1001 Potrero Ave., Building 30, 1st floor
(415) 206-3114
http://sfghdean.ucsf.edu/barnett/default.asp

Only staff and faculty can check materials out of the library, but the public is welcome to come learn, browse, and make copies to their heart's content. The library shelves 3,000 medical books and subscriptions to more than 300 current medical journals. Take advantage of librarian-guided use of online databases and special collections on bioterrorism, the flu vaccine, SARS, and other subjects.

Bureau of Jewish Education Jewish Community Library
Main location: 1835 Ellis St. (on the campus of the Jewish Community High School of the Bay); (415) 567-3327
Jewish Community Center location: 3200 California St.; (415) 292-1254
www.bjesf.org/library.htm

Holding more than 20,000 books, DVDs, CDs, and other media that chronicle every multifaceted angle of Judaism and Jewish life and culture, these 2 library locations foster book groups, community and arts events, lectures, and many more free events.

California College of the Arts Libraries
Simpson Library, 1111 8th St.; (415) 703-9574
Meyer Library, 5212 Broadway, Oakland; (510) 594-3658
http://library.cca.edu

If you're seeking inspirational imagery or want to brush up on the arts, perhaps the combined collection of 53,000 books; 12,000 periodicals; 2,000-plus videos; and about 160,000 slides will give your left brain something to work with. Meyer is the main branch and likely of most use, as it's the college's oldest, predating the SF branch by about 80 years. The public cannot take materials out, but copies are just a dime, and you're welcome to browse freely.

California Historical Society's Research Collections
678 Mission St.
(415) 357-1848
www.californiahistoricalsociety.org

The Catch: The collection offers only limited drop-in hours: Wed through Fri, noon to 4:30 p.m.

From the early explorations of the state to events of the present day, this tremendous collection of photographs, manuscripts, maps, and historical texts is made available to all who seek it. The society boasts 35,000 printed materials plus thousands of images in entertaining and old-timey formats. Bonus find: A historical collection of street images, listed by name, is a great way to look into SF's colorful past.

California Pacific Medical Center's Health and Healing Library
2040 Webster St.
(415) 600-3681
www.cpmc.org/services/ihh/hhc/ihhlibrary

The hospital claims that this is one of the largest public health and medical libraries in the country, and it has been in the information circulation business since 1981. Anyone seeking data on health and well-being, whether that be traditional Western studies or complementary medicine, is welcome to learn from the vast collection of 5,000 titles, videos and audiotapes, and computer access to scores of recent studies and medical journals. On the third Thurs of the month, from 10 to 11 a.m., anyone can take advantage of a librarian-led orientation on how to use the library's holdings most efficiently.

Center for Sex and Culture Library
1519 Mission St.
(415) 902-2071
www.centerforsexandculture.org

The Catch: This library does not offer drop-in hours at this time. Call to schedule an appointment to see the collection. Free, but donations are accepted.

Though not a lending library, this facility offers a browsable collection of pulp erotica, thesis and academic work on sex and sexuality, textbooks, and more—about 2,500 items at last count. The mission of this umbrella organization is to facilitate the study of sexuality and eroticism, thus most reasonable requests will strive to be fulfilled.

Helen Crocker Russell Library of Horticulture
San Francisco Botanical Garden at Strybing Arboretum
1115 Irving St.
(415) 661-1316
www.sfbotanicalgarden.org

With 27,000 volumes and 450 garden periodicals sprouting from its fertile soil, this free horticultural library, open since 1972, is an invaluable resource for any enthusiast with a green (or black) thumb. It's open 7 days a week. You can drop in anytime to try to find solutions to queries on pest management, garden design, ethnobotany, and much more.

Holt Labor Library
4444 Geary Blvd., Suite 207
(415) 387-5700
www.holtlaborlibrary.org

The Catch: Appointments to view the collection are recommended.

Labor activists and the public at large are welcome to utilize this noncirculating historical collection of the political and social movement, including 4,500 books (with an emphasis on Trotskyism); thousands of pamphlets, flyers, and brochures; current and historical periodicals; and other media that carry the message, including videos and DVDs.

J. Paul Leonard Library, San Francisco State University
1630 Holloway Ave.
(415) 338-1854
www.library.sfsu.edu

The Catch: $45 a year to become a Friend of the Library; call (415) 338-2408 or visit www.library.sfsu.edu/general/fol.html for complete instructions and a list of borrower restrictions.

The public is welcome to view this extensive university's collections for free, but if you want to check something out, or take advantage of a host of other library features and services, you must be a paying member. This facility also offers a rich map and atlas collection and a large special collection on the labor movement and labor activity.

J. Porter Shaw Library
At the San Francisco Maritime National Historic Park
Fort Mason Center (Buchanan Street and Marina Boulevard), Building E, 3rd floor
(415) 561-7080
www.nps.gov/safr/historyculture/library-collections.htm

This 17,000-foot facility is primarily a place to study, but it's certainly not without its charms for the seafaring fans of Pacific maritime history among us. The Shaw Library boasts 2 oral history/sea chantey listening rooms for the audio collection of 1,000-plus, and facilities for viewing film and videos. Print materials include 100 years of all of the local newspapers, vessel registries, more than 32,000 volumes, and photocopying services. None of their material leaves the premises, but it's free to look.

Prelinger Library
301 8th St., Room 215
(415) 252-8166
www.prelingerlibrary.org
Open Wed 1 to 8 p.m., some Sun, and by appointment

This private collection, open to the public at no cost on Wed from 1 to 8 p.m., is an impressive general interest resource of books, ephemera, and periodicals. Its charms come from its unique organizational structure that welcomes browsing and throws Dewey decimal to the curb. Subject areas are simply limited to the 4 areas of landscape and geography, media and representation, historical consciousness, and political narratives beyond the mainstream. They specialize in the weird and the off-center and take pride in serving an imagecentric, wordsmithing, and artistic clientele. Note that this is a labor of love, and that drop-in hours can change suddenly and without warning. It's smart to check the current schedule before a visit.

Public Libraries

Main Branch, 100 Larkin St.; (415) 557-4400; www.sfpl.lib.ca.us

Branch Libraries

Anza, 550 37th Ave.; (415) 355-5717

Bayview/Anna E. Waden, 5075 3rd St.; (415) 822-2605

Bernal Heights, 500 Cortland St.; (415) 355-2810

Chinatown, 1135 Powell St.; (415) 355-2888

Eureka Valley/Harvey, 1 José Sarria Ct. (16th Street near Market); (415) 355-5616

Excelsior, 4400 Mission St. (at Cotter); (415) 355-2868

Glen Park, 653 Chenery St.; (415) 355-2858

Golden Gate Valley, 1801 Green St.; (415) 355-5666

Ingleside, 1649 Ocean Ave.; (415) 355-2898

Marina, 1890 Chestnut St.; (415) 355-2823

Merced, 155 Winston Dr.; (415) 355-2825

Mission, 300 Bartlett St.; (415) 355-2800

Mission Bay, 960 4th St.; (415) 355-2838

Noe Valley/Sally Brunn, 451 Jersey St.; (415) 355-5707

North Beach, 2000 Mason St.; (415) 355-5626

Ocean View, 345 Randolph St.; (415) 355-5615

Ortega, 3223 Ortega St.; (415) 504-6053

Park, 1833 Page St.; (415) 355-5656

Parkside, 1200 Taraval St.; (415) 355-5770

Portola, 2450 San Bruno Ave.; (415) 355-5660

Potrero, 1616 20th St.; (415) 355-2822

Presidio, 3150 Sacramento St.; (415) 355-2880

Richmond/Senator Milton Marks, 351 9th Avenue; (415) 355-5600

Sunset, 1305 18th Ave.; (415) 355-2808

Visitacion Valley, 45 Leland Ave.; (415) 355-2848

West Portal, 190 Lenox Way; (415) 355-2886

Western Addition, 1550 Scott St.; (415) 355-5727

Public Library Bookmobiles

Branch Library Improvement Program Bookmobile, (415) 557-4343; call for schedule.

Children's Bookmobile, (415) 557-4344; Mon through Thurs only; call for location schedule.

Public Library of Science
1160 Battery St.
(415) 624-1200
www.plos.org

This nonprofit collection is mission driven by physicians and scientists to make recent works of scientific and medical literature widely available. You can visit the physical street location for free—but everything they publish is available, worldwide and with attribution, through their website.

San Francisco Law Library
401 Van Ness Ave., Room 400 (main library and main location); (415) 554-6821
685 Market St., Suite 420; (415) 882-9310
400 McAllister St., Room 512 (San Francisco Courthouse); (415) 551-3647
www.sfgov.org/site/sfll_index.asp

Everyone should have free access to the materials they need to protect their legal rights, and this city-run facility strives to provide those tools to all who seek them. Not only will the staff teach you how to research difficult topics, such as docket research and local municipal code, but they also provide aspiring legal eagles with online and on-site librarian assistance and a plethora of digital database resources. Geared toward a lay audience, the awesome self-help page is a great resource for those beginning to navigate a course in the legal system.

San Francisco Performing Arts Library and Museum
401 Van Ness Ave., Veteran's Building, 4th floor
(415) 255-4800
www.sfpalm.org

The SFPALM collects and makes available historical documents that chronicle performing arts in the Bay Area and beyond from the gold rush to the present. They boast over two million items of various media in their archives, including items from the San Francisco symphony, opera, ballet, and much more. They are a nonprofit organization with roots going back more than 60 years, and today, in addition to their physical holdings, they offer a host of events and exhibitions, for pay, that showcase themed aspects of their collection.

Sierra Club's William E. Colby Memorial Library
(415) 977-5506
www.sierraclub.org/library

The Catch: Access is free, but appointments are a must.

This noncirculating reference collection is searchable either online or at its SF location, which is chock-full of books, periodicals, mountaineering journals, government documents, historic photographs, slides, maps, and memorabilia.

Sutro Library, a Division of the California State Library
480 Winston Dr.
(415) 731-4477
www.lib.state.ca.us

Though mainly a research tool serving Sacramento-area government officials, our local location contains genealogical and family history imagery and documents for all 50 states, including local history, and rare book and manuscript collections formed by Adolph Sutro. Any information from any library in the system can be sent here. The staff is incredibly helpful, and the entire catalog can be searched online at the URL above.

University of California at San Francisco Libraries
Parnassus, 530 Parnassus Ave.; (415) 476-2334
Mission Bay Library at the Community Center, 1675 Owens St., Room 150;
(415) 514-4060
www.library.ucsf.edu

The Catch: $40 ($20 for students with ID) for 6 months' access.

It's free for the public to come and peruse the library's extensive holdings of health and medical files, including the special Tobacco Control Archives, but users must pay to check out a book and become an active library member—$40 for 6 months. Note that books may be limited, but that the reference collections of medical texts, periodicals, and journals are extensive. Online search tools are well kept and helpful, and on-site study rooms and computer labs that are available to the public are an added bonus (and cheaper than your local coffee shop when you add up the cost of 6 months of lattes).

PETS:
FREE-ROAMING FINDS

*"Money will buy you a fine dog,
but only love can make it wag its tail."*

—RICHARD FRIEDMAN

Fido and Fifi deserve the best. However, they're stuck with a cheapskate like you, so second best will have to suffice. While some pampered pets lay atop plush velvet pillows that their owners paid too much for, your little darlings will still know that you love them if they're adorned with a secondhand collar and a comfy bed of used carpet squares. OK, maybe that's too low rent, but that doesn't mean a responsible caregiver can't save a few bucks while trying to give the best to our furry friends. Here are a few tips that will leave you with more leftover cash for kibble.

City of Berkeley Spay Neuter Your Pet (SNYP)
The Berkeley Animal Care Shelter
2013 2nd St., Berkeley
(510) 981-6600
www.ci.berkeley.ca.us/animalservices/SNYPvoucherprog.html

Because the city values pet control over profits, any pet owner in the city of Berkeley may have his or her animal fixed—just $25 for dogs and $15 for cats. Participants must call a participating veterinarian for a voucher and then bring their animal to the shelter for the surgery. Prearrangements are necessary.

The East Bay Society for the Prevention of Cruelty to Animals
8323 Baldwin St., Oakland
(510) 569-1606
www.eastbayspca.org

Keep your eyes on the website, as this organization has a lot to offer the cash-poor pet-loving community. There's a regular pet loss support group as well as free classes in pet first aid. A handful of days a year, they offer the very popular free shot days, where anyone can come for canine and feline vaccinations and microchips at whatever donation they can afford (or not). The organization donates crates and flat collars (rather than chains) as needed. The regular pet services in the veterinary clinic are stupendous, available to all pets and owners, and dirt cheap—with visits starting at just $30 and vaccines at $15 each. Another Oakland locale is at 410 Hegenberger Loop (510-639-7387). Pit bulls and feral cats are always spayed for free!

Fix Our Ferals

(510) 433-9446

www.fixourferals.org

The Catch: Reservations are a must. Full instructions for animal care are a bit complicated; it's best to read them all on the website. They will not treat any animal with a collar.

Granted, feral animals aren't exactly pets, but they can become pets perhaps, and arguably their well-being means that your pet kitty is better protected from disease and other hazards of overpopulation. Thus, this nonprofit organization serving Alameda and Contra Costa Counties will spay or neuter any wild, trapped cat that you bring in. They'll give feline vaccines and any sort of necessary medical treatment, such as for minor wounds and parasites. They'll even allow you to borrow traps to get the cats in for treatments.

Pet Personals

Not everyone is as responsible as you are, and people part with their animals all the time. Their loss, however, could mean your gain. Whether you like 'em tall and lean or short and chunky, your ideal furry or feathered friend awaits. But however shall you meet? These local and national resources are your best bets for the perfect pet:

Craigslist.org has a pets section, but buyers should beware of truly finding a "purebred" anything.

Petfinder.org is an extremely thorough national resource that allows pet seekers to find their soul mate with a succinct list of search criteria. Browsers can hunt based on species, breed, age, and zip code, just to name a few, and peruse adoptable pets from numerous local rescue groups all at once.

Petco
1685 Bryant St.; (415) 863-1840
1591 Sloat Blvd.; (415) 665-3700
www.luvmypet.com

National low-cost vaccine company Luv My Pet sets up shop in pet stores in 23 states across the country and offers packages of vaccines for dogs, cats, puppies, and kittens for less than most veterinarians—usually around $50 to $60 for several shots. They have locations throughout the Bay Area, but the above locations feature the low-cost vaccines most Saturdays or Sundays. The schedule sometimes changes, so contact the location nearest you.

Pet Food Express
1975 Market St.; (415) 431-4567
3160 20th Ave.; (415) 759-7777
1101 University Ave., Berkeley; (510) 540-7777
5144 Broadway, Oakland; (510) 654-8888
6398 Telegraph Ave., Oakland; (510) 923-9500
www.happypet.com

This monster retailer features low-priced weekend vet care at all of its Northern California locations; a regular regimen of vaccines for cats or dogs costs around $40. In addition, this retailer offers microchipping, blood and fecal testing, flea and tick control, ear mite treatment, deworming, and heartworm prevention through a traveling, mobile clinic. Though nothing can replace the attentive care of regular vet visits, this is a good way to save a few bucks and shop for kibble and squeaky balls at the same time.

San Francisco Society for the Prevention of Cruelty to Animals
2500 16th St.
(415) 554-3000
www.sfspca.org

The main draw here is the Spay and Neuter Clinic, which performs the service on your dog or cat for around $100—cheaper than most private vets. Additionally, the SFSPCA offers low-cost health-care services for pets of seniors and the homeless, plus no-interest loans for pets that require emergency services. If you're seeking pet-friendly housing, they keep a list of landlords who will allow you and your four paws on premises, available gratis. And in the terrible and unlikely event that you'll ever need it, they also offer a free weekly pet loss support group for affected families.

SECTION 3:

Exploring San Francisco

TRANSPORTATION:
ON THE ROAD AGAIN

*"Everywhere is within walking distance
if you have the time."*

—STEVEN WRIGHT

Planes, trains, and wheels—San Francisco's 7 by 7 miles of terrain aren't much to traverse geographically, but when every nook and cranny is packed with so much to see and do, you'll want to cover as much of it as you can—and get around as cheaply, and with as much freedom, as possible. The city is well served by the MUNI bus system (though there are plenty of exceptions to this rule, depending on location, time of day, and all-too-frequent breakdowns), but it's not uncommon for the wait for the bus and the bus ride itself to take the same amount of time as walking. With a little insider know-how, fore-thought, and a bit of luck, one can see this town hobo-style—totally free, or for cheaper than the average price.

PUBLIC **TRANSPORTATION**

Bay Area Rapid Transit (BART)
www.bart.gov/tickets/types/types.asp

BART does not offer weekly or monthly passes for regular East Bay–bound commuters unless you are a school-age student, disabled, or over age 65. Those who take BART within the city may benefit from the purchase of a half-monthly BART Plus Ticket, which allows for transport on MUNI and the San Francisco BART stations and many other Bay Area transportation systems.

Blue and Gold Fleet
www.blueandgoldfleet.com

The Catch: Tickets are only good Mon through Fri, catering to a mostly commuter audience. If you're visiting the area or if you have tourists in town to entertain, check out the periodic Internet specials.

Though mainly a tour operator on the water and on land, this company also offers a small amount of commuter ferries, like those between San Francisco and Sausalito and Tiburon to the north. Web-only specials run periodically that allow for the purchase of 20 regular adult tickets for just $100—a sub-stantial savings of $70 off purchasing individual adult tickets at the $8.50 retail price.

Caltrain
www.caltrain.com/schedule_tickets.html

Travelers commuting mainly to the South Bay can buy a monthly pass and a 10-ride pass, but it's unlikely they'll save much money unless they take more than 10 rides per week. However, those connecting with the Santa Clara Valley Transport Authority or SamTrans with a two-zone ticket can transfer onto a bus on either system for free. Regular San Francisco MUNI riders can add a MUNI sticker to their monthly Caltrain pass for just $40—which is $5 off the price of a regular MUNI Fast Pass alone.

Golden Gate Ferry
http://goldengateferry.org/fareprograms/cashfares.php

The Catch: Discount ticket books expire in 6 months. Use 'em or lose 'em.

Both a bus system and a ferry serving Marin County to the north and its onslaught of commuters who come into SF every day, the ferry offers discount programs to save the working person a few dollars as he or she crosses counties. Ride Value Discount Ticket Books offer 20 percent off the regular price of a one-way adult ferry ticket for boats that run between SF's Ferry Building and Marin's Larkspur and Sausalito. Books must be purchased in packs of 20. Half-off tickets are also available for youths under age 17, those over 65, and people with disabilities. This is one of the most economical ways in the area to get your landlubbing self a 30- to 45-minute ride on the beautiful bay.

Save Money & Time with FasTrak

Owning a car is expensive in San Francisco, no matter how you slice it. Yet there are a couple of ways to save a few bucks when it comes to coughing up for bridge toll. With the handy **FasTrak pass** (www .bayareafastrak.org), one can traverse the Golden Gate Bridge for a buck less (just $4), though shuffling east on the Bay Bridge remains the same price as those who don't have the windshield-affixed tag ($3). Hybrid drivers and those vehicles with 3 passengers or more during rush hour get passage totally free. The best part? No more scrounging for change and dollars in the ashtray.

San Francisco Municipal Railway (MUNI)
www.sfmuni.com

Love it, hate it—no matter how you feel about it, everyone rides San Francisco's favorite (and only) bus and light-rail system. Though its quality and reliability ebbs and flows, the price keeps going up and up—but luckily there are ways to save a few dollars while getting around town. Regular riders will benefit from a weekly pass for just $15 (at a buck and a half a ride, this breaks basic commuters even). Better yet, buy the Fast Pass for $45 before the first of the month to take full advantage of free rides on both MUNI and BART and SamTrans (in SF only). Discounts are also available for youth, the elderly, and the disabled. Purchasing locations are listed on the website.

Always take a transfer. When boarding a bus on street level, it pays to flash today's transfer casually to the driver—even if the time has expired. More often than not, you can get the ride for free. Don't bother trying this tactic riding the lettered trains that board underground. For some reason, these MUNI operators take their job very seriously, and it's likely they won't let you through the gate. Note that this isn't official policy, so you didn't hear this trick from us . . .

TO & **FROM** THE **AIRPORT**

San Francisco International (SFO)
806 South Airport Blvd.
(800) 435-9736
www.flysfo.com

For free information about your transportation options in and out of the airport, dial *1121 from any courtesy phone on premises at the airport, or 511 from any regular telephone.

PUBLIC TRANSPORTATION

BART

The train goes directly into SFO's domestic terminal, and this is certainly your cheapest route to meet your plane—short of begging a new lover to drive you down. This train connects with all of BART's usual stations throughout San Francisco and the East Bay. Costs vary depending on the length of your trip, but one-way from SF's Mission and 16th Streets station is $8.05. To view a schedule and calculate the cost of your trip, visit www.bart.gov or call (650) 992-2278. Note that the BART train also connects passengers with the Caltrain system at Milbrae, serving the South Bay, including Palo Alto and Gilroy.

SamTrans

This also connects the airport with the public transportation system of San Mateo 24 hours a day, including routes KX, 292, and 397. Routes 292 and 397 also stop at SFO's Rental Car Center and the United Airlines Maintenance Center. For more information visit www.samtrans.com or call (800) 660-4287.

Door-to-Door Shuttles Serving SFO

The Catch: Reservations are necessary to get you to the airport, but not necessary upon leaving SFO.

Particularly for passengers traveling alone with too much luggage to carry on their own, this is the next most affordable option in and out of the airport. Prices hover around $20 per passenger one-way. To find these vans at SFO, simply go up one level from Baggage Claim and follow the signs for door-to-door transportation. Expect most of these shysters to try to pack the van for the maximum number of riders; it's not uncommon for the driver to make four or five stops at various locations all over the city, particularly on your way home.

Advanced Airport Shuttle, (650) 504-6641
Airport Express, (415) 775-5121
American Airporter Shuttle, (415) 202-0733, (800) 282-7758
Bay Shuttle, (415) 564-3400
Lorrie's Airport Shuttle, (415) 334-9000
M & M Luxury Shuttle, (415) 552-3200

Pacific Airport Shuttle, (415) 681-6318

Peter's Airport Shuttle, (650) 577-8858

Quake City Shuttle, (415) 255-4899, (415) 621-2831

San Francisco City Shuttle, (888) 850-7878

SuperShuttle, (415) 558-8500

Taxis

Follow the signs out of Baggage Claim toward the taxi stand. Taxis in and out of SFO run around $40 to $50 one-way, and passengers pay the metered fare. Oddly enough, for two or more passengers, this is not much more expensive than paying for a door-to-door shuttle van service (such as Super Shuttle, M & M, and Quake City, most of which usually cost around $15 to $20 per person, plus tip), and a cab will get you there a whole lot quicker. If you are a lone traveler leaving the airport during regular hours and you'd like to split the cost of the trip with a stranger, it pays to walk up to the line and ask if anyone is heading in your same direction. If you're both going toward adjacent neighborhoods in SF and you both have cash, it's a good idea to share the cost of the ride. Request a green cab—won't cost you any more green, but you'll feel better about your carbon footprint.

Oakland International Airport

1 Airport Dr., Oakland

(510) 577-5812

www.flyoakland.com

PUBLIC TRANSPORTATION

AC Transit

For the price of regular bus fair (around $2), East Bay residents can ride directly to the airport on bus lines 50 and N. The N line also runs directly into SF's downtown Transbay Terminal, though the route is pretty slow. Some hours are limited, and some additional fares may apply. Learn more at www.actransit.org or (800) 448-9790.

BART/AirBART

Every 10 to 20 minutes all day, except for late at night, BART riders can transfer at the Coliseum Station to catch the AirBART, which will take them directly to the airport for $2 on top of the price of the regular BART fare. For more information go to www.bart.gov or call (510) 465-BART.

Door-to-Door Shuttle Services Serving SF and the East Bay

Since Oakland is a smaller airport, it costs more to get there, despite the fact that it's not much farther away. Expect to pay about $35 per person, one-way, to ride one of these shuttle services.

A-1 Express Shuttle Service, (888) 676-0565
Acropolis Airport Shuttle, (510) 827-5894
Air-Transit Shuttle, (510) 568-3434
American Airport Shuttle, (415) 202-0733
American Shuttle Express, (408) 259-9500
Angel Express, (866) 295-3797
Apollo Shuttle, (925) 755-8892
Avon Airporter Express, (888) 592-2866
B.A.B.E.S. Airporter, (510) 317-6983
Bay Airporter Express, (510) 234-9759
Bay Area Shuttle, (510) 324-3000
Bay Shuttle, (415) 564-3400
Bay Transit Shuttle, (510) 714-4000
Bayporter Express, (415) 467-1800
Best Way Shuttle, (925) 363-7711
Bridge Airporter, (510) 867-1476
City Express Shuttle, (888) 874-8885
Citywide Shuttle, (510) 816-8569
E-Z Ride Airporter, (510) 393-5554
Flying Eagle Shuttle, (510) 259-0095
Horizon Airporter, (510) 333-4778
Lucky Shuttle, (510) 303-8772
Luxor Shuttle, (510) 562-7222
Quake City Shuttle Inc., (415) 255-4899
Safety Express Shuttle, (510) 388-2029
Shuttle Pro, (866) 499-2447
Silicon Valley Airporter, (650) 869-4476
Silverline Airporter, (510) 259-8609
Super Shuttle, (800) 258-3826
Take Me Home Express, (510) 652-8700
Traveler Shuttle, (510) 909-0965

Tri City Airport Shuttle, (510) 812-3324
USA Shuttle, (510) 744-0222
US Airporter, (510) 223-1228

Taxis

A private car to and from Oakland airport runs around $60 to $65 between the airport and SF. Since the crowd tends to be smaller, sharing one with a stranger is a trickier task.

Campus Yellow Cab, (510) 644-4455
Friendly Cab, (510) 536-3000
Oakland Yellow Cab, (510) 658-2222
Yellow Airport Taxi, (510) 594-1333
Yellow Cab Airport Service, (510) 594-0101

BICYCLES

It's a means of transportation; it's a vehicle for social change. Whether you bike around town for recreation or rely on two wheels for your daily commute, these places can help make your ride smoother.

Bike Hut at South Beach

Pier 40 (Embarcadero and Townsend)
(415) 543-4335
www.thebikehut.com

Here bicycles in the South of Market area can be rented, repaired, and sold while bringing needed funds and social skills to the strata of the population who need it most, as this shop works with local nonprofit and job skills organizations. Bikes rent for as little as $5 an hour and are sold for as little as $40. Check them out for some of the best-priced deals on two wheels.

Craigslist

http://sfbay.craigslist.org/bik/

How many times can we list this bulletin board as a resource? Only when it really is the shopper's best bet for cheap stuff. And if you're looking for a cool bike that's not too "hot," if you know what we mean, this is one of the most affordable bike "shops" in town. Buyer beware, but you can ride away with a great bargain on two wheels.

Missing Link Bicycle Cooperative
1988 Shattuck Ave., Berkeley
(510) 843-7471
www.missinglink.org

For 30 years this 20-or-so member co-op has been keeping the pedal-friendly East Bay moving through a collaboration of low-cost bikes for sale and a community outreach program that offers free loaner tools to do your own bike repair. The free classes will teach you how to do it. There's also a fairly priced repair shop, used bikes for purchase, a calendar of community rides, and more.

Pedal Revolution
3085 21st St.
(415) 641-1264
www.pedalrevolution.com

Yes, it's retail, but it's also a nonprofit organization and oh so much more. In addition to selling new bikes, Pedal offers a great selection of secondhand and refurbished models at fair prices, new and used parts, and professional bike repair. This organization provides employment opportunities and teaches real-world career skills to kids ages 14 to 21 interested in bicycling and bike repair. For $30 a year, those who want to fix their own bikes, but lack the tools and space to do it, can schedule access to Pedal's many workbenches and use their

Plan It More, Pedal Less
If you're trying to build the kind of thigh muscles that turn heads, then feel free to ride San Francisco's endless, steep hills to your heart's content. But if you'd just like to commute around town as safely, effortlessly, and as stress free as possible, take advantage of **Bicycling.511.org,** a free, online collection of interactive bicycling maps and bike route planners. Your quads will thank you.

tools while hitting up staff for assistance (when available). Periodically they offer free workshops for members and nonmembers that will teach you to fix your bike yourself. Beat that, cheapskate!

San Francisco Bike Kitchen
650H Florida St.
www.bikekitchen.org

Even cheaper than Pedal Revolution, this DIY repair shop provides the space and resources to let you fix your own two-wheeled steed for just $5 a day or $30 per year. But even if you can't afford the fee for services, a few hours of volunteering will buy you the same access in trade. Deep lovers of bicycling can volunteer to start earning a bike frame and parts to build their own rig. Inquire about their house Earn-a-Bike program for those with lots of time and enthusiasm but short on cash. Fee-based classes are offered on premises that teach the basics of bike building and bike repair.

Street Level Cycles
84 Bolivar Dr., Berkeley
www.watersideworkshops.org/slc/

This full-service community bike shop near the Berkeley marina offers cyclists access to a free do-it-yourself repair studio. On Tues and Thurs between 2 and 6 p.m., and Sat and Sun between noon and 6 p.m., bring your bike in and use all the tools you could possibly need to get your ride back on the road, free of charge. Friendly staff members are extremely knowledgeable and happy to help you with your repair. The shop also has a great selection of used bicycles for sale, and buying here supports a youth-education program (you'll often see teenagers tinkering away at their beloved wheels—a precious site to behold).

PUBLIC ART, GARDENS & ATTRACTIONS:
SHOW ME THE MONET

"If wealth is found by rejecting the experience of poverty, then it will never be complete. The soul is nurtured by want as much as by plenty."

—THOMAS MOORE

Beauty is in the eye of the beholder, and when beauty is being given away for free, art is all that much more ravishing. San Francisco is a stunning city with loads of vistas that are easy on the eyes, but when the cranial sensibilities crave a bit of man-made sophistication, the city's bustling arts scene is a bounty of entertainment. From fast street art to the slicked-up MoMA, from the careful cultivation of a well-sculpted garden to the plethora of galleries and museums that dot the neighborhoods, the well-planned lover of aesthetics will feast. Visitors and locals alike cannot overlook the streamlined eye candy of some of San Francisco's sauciest and best-known landmarks, such as the Dr. Seuss-y twist of Lombard Street, our pretty painted Victorian ladies, or the colorful swath of the Golden Gate Bridge. They are proof that art is everywhere, and that creative expression courses through our metropolitan veins.

WALKING **TOURS**

Strap on your fancy footwear and pack the binoculars. We've got a city to conquer.

Barbary Coast Trail
www.sfhistory.org

The San Francisco Museum and Historical Society has put together this interesting, free, 4-mile self-guided walking tour ripe with city history. It covers 20 historical sites of interest, stunning views, and beautiful main streets and side alleys in a handful of diverse neighborhoods. While whole books are available that detail the finer points of every stop, bare-bones information and a printable map are available on the website above for the public to download at will.

City Guides Walking Tours
www.sfcityguides.org

The Catch: This is sponsored by the public library, but a donation envelope is passed at the end with a request for funds to keep the program going. Cash is requested but not required.

From brothels to hotels, from whole neighborhoods to San Francisco's forests and murals, this outstanding resource offers a busy calendar of free ways to access the history and lore of our fair city on your own two feet, and it's a popular pastime for visitors and local residents alike. Volunteer tour leaders are a font of knowledge on their particular subject matter as well as city history, and many of them share firsthand and personal knowledge and experience as well.

On The Level SF
www.onthelevelsf.com

Let's face it—San Francisco is a topographical destination, but one that's not easily navigable by everyone. Sometimes shorter, accessible walking tours (without hills!) are a necessity even for folks who have walking stamina. People with some limited mobility will rejoice to find this collection of free, self-guided walking tours that explore some of the area's most interesting neighborhoods. While this company does offer some services that cost money—such as guided tours or tours that involve meals—anyone can go to the website and download the information on self-guided tours to destinations like Golden Gate Park and the Marina Green.

San Francisco Botanical Garden at Strybing Arboretum
9th Avenue (at Lincoln Way), Golden Gate Park
(415) 661-1316, ext. 312
www.sfbotanicalgarden.org

While California budget cuts have left this once-free slice of naturalistic heaven a paying affair, SF residents (with ID to prove it) get in free, and for others it's still well worth the $7; and it's free for everyone on the second Tuesday of every month! Trained and knowledgeable garden-loving docents offer daily, totally free tours of this exemplary botanical garden at 1:30 p.m. Anyone with a green thumb should snatch up this opportunity. Those who prefer to trod the green path solo can download a walking map from the website or pick up a self-guided brochure on-site.

San Francisco City Hall Tours
1 Dr. Carlton B. Goodlett Place, Room 008
Office of the Building General Manager
(415) 554-4933
www.sfgov.org
Mon through Fri, 10 a.m., noon, and 2 p.m.

The massive, golden rotunda in San Francisco's Civic Center is truly a sight to behold, and those interested in this architectural masterpiece of Arthur Brown Jr. and John Bakewell Jr. will enjoy the daily, free 45-minute guided tours of one of city government's most interesting and talked-about buildings. Visitors must sign up for tours at the information/tour kiosk near the front door. Private tours can be arranged in advance for larger groups (though the often requires a small fee). School groups go free.

San Francisco Parks Trust Park Guides
(415) 263-0991
www.sfpt.org

Golden Gate Park is perhaps our city's best resource, from city statues to the historic Japanese Tea Garden, from stroller walks to the AIDS Grove. Locals and visitors should not squander this free opportunity to get to know one of the city's largest parks more intimately. Educated guides will take you on walking tours from windmill to windmill or lake to lake, and best of all, it's unlikely they will get you lost—quite a feat among the park's numerous twisty paths and turns. These tours are your city's tax dollars at work for something great.

MURALS

An empty wall is just a white canvas for San Francisco's many artists. We're not talking about graffiti here: These murals are requested, planned, and exquisitely executed. On a sunny day a mural tour is one of the best ways to view the entire city as a gallery.

BALMY ALLEY & 24TH STREET
In the heart of the Mission District, this alleyway is filled top to bottom and side to side with murals in conversation with one another and with the alley's topography, cultural iconography, and the city's global history. Balmy Alley is at once breathtaking and illuminating, depicting political struggle, Latin American cultural heroes, and so much more.

Beach Chalet

1000 Great Hwy.
(415) 386-8439
http://beachchalet.com

It took two years to paint, but the glorious and colorful depictions inside this historic building at the edge of Golden Gate Park and Ocean Beach were well worth the effort. Artist Lucien Labaudt toiled tirelessly to capture the images and sensations of San Francisco during the Great Depression, and he captured every corner of the city in the process, from Fisherman's Wharf to South of Market. Also on display in the lobby: more historic memorabilia and an excellent model of Golden Gate Park. While you're here, pop into the restaurant upstairs for a cocktail and a great ocean view.

Broadway Tunnel Mural

Broadway and Polk Street

Basically just a utilitarian thoroughfare from Russian Hill to Chinatown and the red light district, this heretofore inconsequential concrete wall has been transformed into a thing of nature-like beauty, thanks to British artist Paul Curtis. Using a high-pressure water gun against the retainer wall leading up to the Broadway tunnel, Curtis erases away decades of the city's grit and exhaust to create a naturescape (worthy of the SF MoMA) that reminds us what used to be in this tunnel's stead. Remarkable to view while passing by in a car or on a bike, you can also sneak a peak from across the street and above the entrance to the tunnel.

CLARION ALLEY & VALENCIA STREET

This alley may not smell so fresh, but its visual allure and fresco designs make it a must-see for fans of folk art and hip-hop alike. Rather than one simple statement, several artists share this long public street, thus the experience is diverse and ever changing. Keep your eyes on the walls for the date of the annual block party, when residents come out to celebrate the latest installations and revel in the overall hipness.

Coit Tower
1 Telegraph Hill
(415) 362-0808

At the bequest of SF socialite and philanthropist Lillie Coit, this popular landmark features spectacular views of the Bay Area on the outside and unforgettable World War II–era political murals inside its large rotunda. Every so often the city considers charging tourists an entrance fee to pay for its preservation, but for now stepping in to view the ground floor is free.

Diego Rivera at the City Club
155 Sansome, 10th floor

This too-posh venue boasts great views and high-class fare, but its true treasure is one of Diego Rivera's first murals commissioned in the United States. Dress to fit in and head on up to the 10th floor and see Diego Rivera's allegorical depiction of Lady California and the struggle between human beings and machines, gold and heart, industry and the natural world. It's sure to take your breath away—but head back downstairs quickly before they kick you out.

Duboce Bikeway Mural
Duboce and Church Streets
www.monacaron.com/murals.html

Mona Caron, the celebrated artist behind the Market Street Railway mural, made her name with this transcendent and dreamy bike-ride depiction of Northern California's best outdoor scenery. Never before has the back of a Safeway supermarket looked so good. MUNI riders are spared what would have undoubtedly been a frequently graffittied concrete wall; instead they ride off into the sunset. Those pressed for time can simply take the J Church or the N Judah past for a quick view, but there's so much detail that the mural is best savored by foot.

MaestraPeace at the Women's Building
3543 18th St.
(415) 431-1180
www.womensbuilding.org

Eyes Wide Open at Precita Eyes

The Mission District is bursting with color and culture, both of which take form in the neighborhood's iconic murals that both boast from buildings and subtly sigh from their space on the street. While just looking is moving enough, the local organization **Precita Eyes** (2981 24th St.; 415-285-2287; www.precitaeyes.org) offers informative mural walks that ground the larger-than-life paintings in a context both cultural and historical. Proceeds from tours go to benefit the educational, outreach, and preservation programs of this long-standing San Francisco institution. Prices range from $8 to $15, which is not cheap. For our money, though, it's well worth the bills.

Finished in 1994, this massive building on a whole square block bursts with a colorful mural that's a multiethnic, multigenerational celebration of women and female roles through the ages. A team of seven women artists joined forces to memorialize female icons and their accomplishments from around the globe.

The Making of a Fresco [Making a Fresco] Showing the Building of a City
At the Art Institute of San Francisco
800 Chestnut St.
(415) 771-7020
www.sanfranciscoart.edu

Famed artist and muralist Diego Rivera crafted this metamural, highlighting the creation of a fresco within a fresco, in 1931. Those who worked with him on the piece are immortalized here. This is one of Rivera's four murals that made their mark on the city. It is the magnet drawing people to the student art gallery, which is open free to the general public.

Market Street Railway Mural
Church and 15th Streets
www.monacaron.com/murals.html

This award-winning newcomer among San Francisco's most notable murals is a multipaneled elapsed time capsule of Market Street through the decades.

Painted on a convenience-store wall, cable cars, automobiles, and pedestrians share visual space on this portrayal of the historic thoroughfare that leads toward an imagined future of sustainable community travel (a very SF dream). It's worthy of more than a casual second glance.

Marriage of the Artistic Expression of the North and of the South on this Continent
(commonly known as *Pan American Unity*)
At City College of San Francisco
50 Phelan Ave.
(415) 239-3000
www.riveramural.org

Mexican goddesses and Indian woodcarvers are the crux of this piece, perhaps SF's most famous mural, painted by Diego Rivera in 1940. This must-see contribution proudly adorns the Diego Rivera Theater, and surely it has inspired more than one student to reach a higher level of excellence. The main theme of the piece is to create a unified America, bringing the continent's central and southern residents into the northern fold.

CEMETERIES & **CREMATORIUMS**

While we, the living, bustle around the bay, its easy enough to forget the city's incredibly rich and diverse history—and for those of us who can get past the creep-factor, San Francisco's cemeteries offer an incredible testament to the city's founders and foundations. Besides serving as the final resting place for all those people we've named our streets after, they are some of the city's most beautiful and pristine spots, quietly paying homage to our diverse populations, culture, and architecture.

The Cemetery at Mission Dolores Basilica
3321 16th St.
(415) 621-8203
www.missiondolores.org

Although this beautiful and historic mission is the final resting place of more than 5,000 American Indians, its cemetery, dating from 1830, commemorates some of San Francisco's most famous names that now adorn street signs, such as Arguello, Frederick, Balboa, and more. These century-old stone markers and their surrounding gardens are truly a sight to behold. While you're here, be sure to tour the historic mission itself, once visited by Pope John Paul II and home to generations of worshippers.

Chapel of the Chimes
4499 Piedmont Ave., Oakland
(510) 654-0123
www.chapelofthechimes.com

It's a crematorium, plus a whole lot more! Visitors will be absolutely enthralled by the unforgettable building designed by Julia Morgan (celebrated American architect of Hearst Castle fame), but there's plenty to do here for the living as well. The site houses regular coffee club gatherings, author readings, and our favorite—Jazz at the Chimes, which is 10 bucks well spent for a weekend afternoon that is so entertaining that people are just dying to get in.

Pet Cemetery at the Presidio
Northwestern corner of San Francisco
(415) 561-4323 (information)
www.nps.gov/prsf

No one seems to know how it started, but an ancient, well-maintained pet burial ground on a military base is absolutely a site worthy of a visit. Here the rodents, dogs, cats, and birds of colonels, generals, and other high-ranking military personnel come to rest, with proper epitaphs and headstones to boot. As in any other sacred final resting place, the intrepid can find several unknown markers—as no one should forget the guinea pig that died in honor of his country.

The San Francisco Columbarium
1 Loraine Ct.
(415) 752-7891

Tucked into SF's Outer Richmond district, this crematorium has about 7,500 "apartments" in which the deceased can rest, but it likely houses the remains of 65,000 inhabitants. Now run by the Neptune Society, the beautiful Victorian building is more than 100 years old and features 3 stories of ancient burial vaults.

The San Francisco National Cemetery

At the Presidio, northwest corner of SF
(415) 561-4323 (information)
www.nps.gov/prsf

More than 30,000 soldiers have been laid to rest here among the 28 acres in the Old Presidio Army Base. The site is part of the National Park Service and the Golden Gate National Recreation Area. The look of the headstones has the understatement of an Arlington National, but the first honorees to be interned here date from 1854. This is the largest remaining cemetery in San Francisco.

PUBLIC GARDENS

Conservatory of Flowers

JFK Drive, Golden Gate Park
(415) 666-7001
www.conservatoryofflowers.org

If you just haven't the time to jet down to Bali or Brazil for a traipse through an enchanted rain forest, this stunning plant collection, viewable on the cheap, is the next best alternative. The rare collection of orchids, brome-liads, carnivorous plants, and other tropical species from around the globe are breathtaking, and even more so for the green thumbed among us. The building itself is not to be missed: The oldest conservatory in the Western Hemisphere dates from 1878 and reopened its doors in 2003 after a vigorous restoration. Be sure to catch their periodic special exhibits, such as "Wicked Plants," a collection of the world's most dangerous plants, and the beautiful butterfly room. Admission is $5, and there's free entry the first Tuesday of the month.

Japanese Tea Garden

Off JFK Drive, Golden Gate Park
(415) 752-4227

It's listed in every tourist guidebook and for good reason: This easy, sculpted stroll through carefully shaped trees, well-appointed stones and bridges, and clear, koi-stocked ponds instantly puts the mind at ease. Since 1894 this has been a showcase for Japanese and Chinese native flora, though the bulk of the plants were donated when their expert collector was shipped off to Japanese internment during World War II. It thus serves as both a celebration of life and somber (if subtle) reminder of a dark spot in our nation's history and is worth a visit anytime—though in summer the tourist foot traffic can make the garden feel as crowded as a Tokyo subway. The shaded teahouse on premises may not be the most authentic, but it's still a lovely place to take a date or whittle away a warm afternoon for just a few dollars. Garden admission is $4, and there's free admission Mon, Wed, and Fri from 9 to 10 a.m.

San Francisco Botanical Garden at Strybing Arboretum
9th Avenue at Lincoln Way, Golden Gate Park
(415) 564-3239
www.sfbotanicalgarden.org

This breathtaking urban oasis of natural beauty features plant species from all over the world, plus a library and free guided walking tours every single day of the year. This fenced-in resource is a pristine, dog-free must-see in one of SF's largest and most populated parks—and a great place to feed the waterfowl to boot. Free admission on Tuesday for non-San Francisco residents, and free every day for locals with an ID that shows you're one of us!

Yerba Buena Gardens
Between 3rd and 4th Streets on Mission Street

OK, essentially this is just a park. But what makes this spot of green worthy of a mention is its location. This is one of the few places where your butt can touch grass in the Downtown area (though technically it's SoMa, but not by much). There's a wonderful fountain to walk beneath where you'll find dramatic stone inscriptions quoting the words of MLK Jr., the memorial fountain's namesake. Short of a spa break on your lunch hour, this is the next best way to rejuvenate and get away from your crappy temp job's bland four walls.

COMMUNITY **GARDENS**

Community Gardens Program
Sponsored by San Francisco Recreation and Parks
(415) 581-2541 (information)
http://parks.sfgov.org

San Francisco has more than 40 small plots of volunteer-run, first come, first served community gardens that are free for public use (though most gardens pool together small sums to cover common expenses). These are lovely to visit, particularly during the growing season, and they're even more fun to cultivate. Look for signs posted around the gardens in your community, as many neighborhoods use these spaces for social gatherings, holiday sales, and more.

Bayview/Hunter's Point: Adam Rogers Park, Ingalls at Oakdale

Bernal Heights: Gates at Banks; Prospect at Courtland; Ogden Terraces, Ogden and Prentiss; Park Street, Park and San Jose

Corona Heights: States at Museum; Crags Court, Crags at Berkeley

Crocker Amazon: Moscow at Geneva; Dublin at Russia

Dogpatch: Brewster at Rutledge

Eureka Valley: Corwin at Douglass

Glen Park: Arlington at Highland

The Haight: Koshland Park Community Learning Garden, Page at Buchanan; Page and Laguna Mini Park

Mission District: Alioto Mini Park, 20th Street at Capp; KidPower Park, 45 Hoff St. at 16th Street; Treat Commons at Parque Ninos Unidos, 23rd Street and Treat; Potrero del Sol, Cesar Chavez and Potrero
Nob Hill: Mason at Pine
Noe Valley: Clipper and Grandview
North Beach: Michelangelo Playground, Greenwich at Jones
Outer Mission: Lessing/Sears Mini Park
Potrero Hill: 25th Street at De Haro; 22nd Street and Arkansas; 22nd Street and Connecticut; 20th Street and San Bruno Avenue
Richmond District: Golden Gate Senior Center; 37th Street at Fulton
South of Market: Howard/Langton Mini Park; Folsom and Sherman
St. Mary's Park: Alemany at Ellsworth
Sunset District: White Crane Springs; South of 7th Avenue and Lawton
Upper Market: Noe/Beaver Mini Park
Visitacion Valley: McLaren Park, Leland at Hahn; Visitacion Valley Greenway, Arleta at Rutland

ART **GALLERIES**

First Thursdays Downtown
www.firstthursdayart.com

Mark your calendars now. On the first Thursday of every month, almost all of the posh Downtown galleries in SF open up their doors after hours to the after-work crowd, and this means free art spying, free scene schmoozing, and lotsa, lotsa free wine and cheese. Most of the galleries are in or around Geary, Post, and Sutter Streets, but all are within a mile of one another on flat, easily walkable streets. You can start anywhere—most stay open until 7:30 p.m. or later—but beginning at the multigalleried 49 Geary space near Market will get you off to a nice start. Nibblers and imbibers can enjoy viewing numerous masters, such as Renoir, Warhol, and Picasso, and many contemporary, lesser known, and local talents as well.

All of these galleries are quite accomplished, but here are a few that are sure to entertain:

Graystone, 77 Geary St.; (415) 956-7693

Hang, 556 Sutter St.; (415) 434-4264; www.hangart.com

Martin Lawrence, 366 Geary St.; (415) 956-0345; www.martinlawrence.com

Weinstein, 383 Geary St.; (415) 362-8151; www.weinstein.com

MISSION GALLERIES

On the opposite end of the spectrum from Downtown, the lovably downscale Mission District is home to another walkable stretch of great galleries for a more accessible (and at times way more interesting) aesthetic. Not only do the pieces rival the polish and sleek that you'll find downtown, but the hip scenesters here to admire it are just way, way cooler. If you are an aspiring cheapskate art collector, note that this part of town probably has more pieces than elsewhere that are under $100. And if you have a sharp eye, you may even find pieces being given away for free, stapled to a lamppost or tied to a bicycle rack.

While there are no regular tours or scheduled open houses that bring all of the galleries together, the neighborhood welcomes browsers at all times. Many of these locations also offer public programs and art classes for disadvantaged and/or art-oriented residents, meaning any contribution you make ups both good-for-the-city programming and your personal store of karma. For an occasional glass of free Yellow Tail and a cube or two of Trader Joe's Monterey Jack, sign up for each individual gallery's mailing list to be kept informed of openings. Here are a few that always deliver:

Blue Room Gallery, 2331 Mission St.; (415) 282-8411

City Art Gallery, 828 Valencia St.; (415) 970-9900; www.cityartgallery.org

Creativity Explored, 3245 16th St.; (415) 863-2108; www.creativity explored.org

Galeria de la Raza, 2857 24th St.; (415) 826-8009; www.galeriadelaraza.org

Intersection for the Arts, 925 Mission St.; (415) 626-2787; www.the intersection.org

66balmy, 66 Balmy Alley; (415) 648-1760

Open Studios

Think of this as Halloween for art lovers, featuring numerous free treats and very few tricks every weekend in October. Nearly every artist in every neighborhood flings the studio doors wide open and invites the public to come peruse not just the display of finished pieces for sale but also all of the paint-splattered, dust-covered spaces where the works were created. Artworks run the gamut from entirely affordable collage, photorealistic paintings, and expressionistic photography to everything in between. And wherever there are art openings, there's snacking. Wine and chocolates and cheese are as plentiful and as eclectic as the hordes of local arts supporters that parade from door to door. Do not miss this annual fall visual arts preview. Find the map detailing the hundreds of participating studios in the *San Francisco Bay Guardian* or online at www.artspan.org.

SOUTH OF MARKET GALLERIES

There's a lot of art SoMa, but most of it is mixed with something more, either as part of a multiuse art space or as part of a bar or restaurant. Each visitor will walk away with his or her own impression—is it a bar with some art on the wall, or is it a gallery that just happens to serve drinks? The region encourages visitors to not be such purists about their visual stimulation—that yes, indeed, that mammoth Brian Barneclo painting does look better with a DJ soundtrack and a blood orange martini or two. Clearly this is not to everyone's taste. But if you like your sculpture shaken and stirred, come here to imbibe, investigate, and get inspired.

The Luggage Store, 1007 Market St.; (415) 255-5971; www.luggagestore gallery.org

111 Minna Gallery, 111 Minna St.; (415) 974-1719; www.111minnagallery .com

SF Camerawork, 657 Mission St., 2nd floor; (415) 512-2020; www.sfcamera work.org

Varnish, 77 Natoma St.; (415) 222-6131; www.varnishfineart.com

ELSEWHERE IN SAN FRANCISCO

Pier 24 Gallery
Pier 24 The Embarcadero
(415) 512-7424
www.pier24.org

Housed in an unassuming old pier-meets-warehouse building, Pier 24 is a private photography collection free and open to the public and sure to knock your socks off. With photography bigwigs like Richard Avedon, Dorothea Lang, Paul Strand, and Bruce Davidson, as well as lesser-known masters, this private collection turned public is a true (free) gift to the city's art lovers.

Recology SF Artist in Residence Program
503 Tunnel Ave.
(415) 330-1415
http://sunsetscavenger.com/AIR/

Some artists claim that they create from thin air, but Recology SF's creatives make art from garbage. Just a handful of artists are fortunate enough to be allowed residency at the dump—that's right, the trash collector—and as such, they have access to all of the discarded waste and recycling material they could ever dream of. The community is invited to see these raw materials in action at several different art openings a year, and the results are always a remarkable makeover. Come early to sneak a peek at the hefty, waste-crunching machinery on-site and to catch an eyeful of the scavenging birds of prey up above. The smells will be memorable. Stiletto pumps are not advised.

San Francisco Arts Commission Gallery
401 Van Ness Ave.
(415) 554-6080
www.sfacgallery.org

In the Civic Center, among the formal sterility of SF's government buildings, this eye in the storm features a consistent stream of excellent work by local artists. While you're in the area applying for your artistic grant, be sure to stop in for a peek.

San Francisco City Hall
1 Carlton B. Goodlett Place, Room 282
(415) 554-7630
www.sfacgallery.org

Also in the Civic Center, this auxiliary SFAC gallery is another spotlight on local talent, and one that's absolutely worth a visit while you're in applying for your marriage license (gay or straight). These exhibits tend to lean more toward the photographic arts.

MUSEUMS

Always Free
Cable Car Museum, 1201 Mason St.; (415) 474-1887; www.cablecarmuseum.org
CCA Wattis Institute for Contemporary Arts, California College of the Arts; 1111 8th St.; www.wattis.org
Chinese Cultural Center of San Francisco, 750 Kearny St., 3rd floor; (415) 986-1822; www.c-c-c.org
GLBT Historical Society, 657 Mission St., #300; (415) 777-5455; www.glbthistory.org
Museo Italo Americano, Fort Mason Center, Building C; (415) 673-2200; www.museoitaloamericano.org.
Octagon House, 2645 Gough St.; (415) 441-7512. Contributions are welcome, and hours are quite limited. It's best to call before planning a visit.
Randall Museum, 199 Museum Way; (415) 554-9600; www.randallmuseum.org
San Francisco Fire Department Museum, 655 Presidio Ave.; (415) 563-4630; www.sffiremuseum.org. Hours are limited; best to call ahead.

Staple Museums with Regular Free Days
Asian Art Museum, 200 Larkin St.; (415) 581-3500; www.asianart.org. Free the first Tuesday of the month. On Thurs after 5 p.m., admission is just $5.
Bay Area Discovery Museum, East Fort Baker, 557 McReynolds Rd., Sausalito; (415) 339-3900; www.baykidsmuseum.org. Free the second Sat of the month after 1 p.m. This is great for kids; worth a drive across the bridge.

California Academy of Sciences (Steinhart Aquarium), 875 Howard St.; (415) 321-8000; www.calacademy.org. Free the first Wednesday of the month. For SF residents looking to beat the crowds (and the cost!), look up your neighborhood's complimentary visit day at www.calacademy.org/visit/sf_free_days_2011.php

Cartoon Art Museum, 655 Mission St.; (415) 227-8666; www.cartoonart .org. The first Tuesday of the month is "pay what you wish" day.

Chinese Historical Society of America Museum and Learning Center, 965 Clay St.; (415) 391-1188; www.chsa.org. Free the first Thursday of the month.

Contemporary Jewish Museum, 121 Steuart St.; (415) 344-8800; www.jmsf .org. Free the third Monday of the month.

de Young Museum, 50 Hagiwara Tea Garden Dr., Golden Gate Park; (415) 863-3330; www.thinker.org. Free the first Tuesday of the month. On Fri after 5 p.m., admission is just $5. Do not miss the view from the top of the tower.

Exploratorium, 3601 Lyon St.; (415) 561-0360; www.exploratorium.edu. Free the first Wednesday of the month.

Legion of Honor, 34th Avenue at Clement Street, Lincoln Park; (415) 863-3330; www.thinker.org. Free the first Tuesday of the month. MUNI riders with a Fast Pass or transfer always receive $2 off regular admission.

Musee Mecanique, Pier 45, Shed A; (415) 346-2000; www.musee mechanique.org. There is no admission fee, but all of the attractions are coin operated. For the truly penny-pinching, enjoyment can be had by enjoying the turn-of-the-20th-century amusements on someone else's quarter. This is especially true of the collection's many player pianos.

Museum of Craft and Folk Art, 51 Yerba Buena Ln.; www.mocfa.org. Free the first Tuesday of the month.

Oakland Museum of California, 1000 Oak St., Oakland; (510) 238-2200. Free the first Sunday of the month.

The Mexican Museum, Fort Mason Center Building D, Marina Boulevard at Buchanan Street; (415) 202-9700; www.mexicanmuseum.org. Free the first Wednesday of the month. Note that at press time, the museum was planning its impending move to a permanent space at Yerba Buena, so check the website for updates.

San Francisco Museum of Craft & Design, 550 Sutter St.; (415) 773-0303; www.sfmcd.org. Free every first Thurs after 5 p.m.

San Francisco Museum of Modern Art, 151 3rd St.; (415) 357-4000; www
.sfmoma.org. Free the first Tuesday of the month, and admission is half
price on Thurs after 6 p.m.

San Francisco Zoo, Sloat Boulevard at Great Highway; (415) 753-7080; www
.sfzoo.org. Free the first Wednesday of the month, with discounts every day
for SF residents with proof of residence.

Yerba Buena Center for the Arts, 701 Mission St.; (415) 978-2700; www
.ybca.org. Free the first Tuesday of the month.

SO **VERY** SF

A view costs nothing—if you know where to find it—and the city's full of
vistas that will knock your darned-up socks off. This is true, as well, of San
Francisco classic experiences that won't cost you a dime but will leave you
feeling well traveled and aesthetically pleased.

de Young Museum's Observation Tower

50 Hagiwara Tea Garden Dr., Golden Gate Park
(415) 863-3330
www.thinker.org

Hands down the best view of the city, with panoramic vistas of every peak
and valley, tree and creature, house and haunt that makes the city famous.
Nestled in Golden Gate Park, the de Young Museum's free-to-visit observa-
tion tower lifts you up and over the trees to remind you where you are and
why you've come.

Elevator of the Hyatt Regency Embarcadero Hotel

5 Embarcadero Center
(415) 433-3717

The foot of Market Street is home to one of the area's best glass elevators.
It soars 17 stories through the mammoth, retro-era atrium. Walk in like you
own the place and take 'em for a spin—you'll be surprised how much it feels
like a roller coaster.

The Golden Gate Bridge

Most folks drive the bridge during their daily commute and forget to notice its beauty, but those who savor life's free bounty should walk this splendid city landmark. Enjoy panoramic bay views of Angel Island, Alcatraz, teams of sailboats, and the statuesque presence of the bridge itself.

The Grace Cathedral Labyrinth

1100 California St.
(415) 749-6300
www.gracecathedral.org

Quiet your mind and take a walk within the lines of this beautiful outdoor attraction. The church itself is quite a lady, but this outdoor path toward enlightenment is open anytime, with a "cool factor" that makes it worth a trip to this very posh neighborhood.

Hyde Street Pier

500 Jefferson St.
(415) 447-5000

Landlubbers can pay $5 to tour the historic vessels that dot this ancient wooden pier, but there's really no need, as a stroll among the ships is totally free.

The Stairways of San Francisco

Rumor has it that SF has more than 300 quirky outdoor staircases connecting our curving, topographically challenged streets. While some such as the Filbert Steps and the Iron Street Stairs are famous as an attraction in their own rights, exploring these hidden gems is a great way to immerse yourself in the city's most intimate nooks and crannies and to see the underside of neighborhoods you might otherwise miss. To find out more about the location and history of these stairways to heaven, check out *Stairway Walks in San Francisco* by Adah Bakalinsky, or visit www.sisterbetty.org/stairways.

Mission Creek Marina
On Berry Street between 4th and 7th Streets

Houseboats? In SF? Indeed, matey. Only the saltiest of urbanites dare habituate the murky waters between lattes. This floating neighborhood houses the only houseboats in the city in an area just bustling with redevelopment.

24th and York Street Mini-Park Snake
It's a play structure, a water fountain, and a very hands-on piece of climbable art. Quetzalcoatl, the mythic feathered sea serpent of the Aztecs, comes to life in this neighborhood park as a breathtaking, Gaudí-esque mosaic sculpture that is one of the most underrated public properties in the 415. Go and check it out.

Twin Peaks View
Heaps of SF's high elevations offer excellent views, but a drive up to the very top of Twin Peaks Boulevard is pure brilliant spectacle, day or night.

The Twisty Streets—Lombard and Vermont
Any guidebook will tell you about the ridiculously corkscrewed section of Lombard (at Hyde) in the Marina that's more like a slope than a street. But those in the know prefer the less-trafficked, less-touristy coiled stretch of Vermont (at 20th Street) in the Portrero for a fun, short drive of a different sort. Both are sure to throw your car's brakes.

ANNUAL EVENTS:
STREET FETES & FREE-FOR-ALLS

*"The mint makes it first, it is
up to you to make it last."*

—EVAN ESAR

In case this book has not made it clear so far, San Francisco is a town that loves to party in the street. Other chapters have mentioned numerous film festivals —and how to get into them for free. We've also covered the myriad outdoor concert events where no ticket is required. But there are plenty more bargains for the socialite penny-pinchers seeking a broad range of activities, and they'd be wise to mark their calendar for these excellent annual events that don't cost nothin' to attend. If you're a big fan of crowds and sunshine—or, depending on the occasion, a fan of fog, men in leather, Jerry Garcia, carnival eats, or floating paper lanterns—then the urgency to celebrate in the "free"dom of the outdoors is an even stronger critical push. Event dates vary from year to year, and this is by no means a comprehensive list, but the following action items for your social calendar will let you party without pay or pity all year long.

JANUARY

Vietnamese Tet Festival
www.vietccsf.org

The Tenderloin comes alight with this street festival of cultural dance and music, so much so that you might, for a moment, forget about the sketchy odors that spur from the neighborhood's streets. Though this seems like an unlikely playground, "Little Saigon" has a lot to offer, including cheap beer and delicious, low-priced *banh mi* and other Vietnamese edible delights. Though this event attracts thousands, it is a smaller, more intimate gathering than many of SF's other street fests.

FEBRUARY

Chinese New Year Festival and Parade
www.chineseparade.com

Chinatown bursts into fireworks throughout the month with a host of cultural events, demonstrations, and even a Miss Chinatown USA pageant. However, the real draw is the massive, glowing, dragon-studded parade that winds and slithers its way around the neighborhood's colorful corners.

MARCH

St. Patrick's Day Parade
www.sfstpatricksdayparade.com

Don your green, but don't plan to spend any. This monstrous celebration of the Irish community is not as huge as some of SF's other parades, but it's always a grand cultural happening and a beer-swilling good time. Behold the beauty of Irish dancing, music, floats, and flag waving.

APRIL

Alternative Press Expo
www.comic-con.org/ape

True, this event does yield a ticket price, but it takes many volunteers to make it happen, and if you work it your efforts will save you the $15 admission fee. And it's worth it—this is among the largest gathering of self-published alternative comics, zines, and graphic novels in the country. Not only are the publications cheap, but also this is a great way to support your favorite starving writers and artists.

Anarchist Bookfair
http://sfbookfair.wordpress.com

Duh—it's anarchists! Of course it's free! And your mind will follow suit. If this is your political bag of media and progressive, culturally fringed crowd watching, you will not be disappointed. This annual gathering has been happening for over a decade, bringing together more than 50 published authors, artists, filmmakers, and more.

Cherry Blossom Festival
www.nccbf.org

This springtime celebration wakes up Japantown from its winter slumber. It features boatloads of music and dance performances and a parade, culinary treats, classes and demonstrations, and much more. Many of the events are totally free.

Opening Day on the Bay
www.picya.homestead.com/OpeningDay.html

The Pacific Inter-Club Yacht Association assembles this vast collection of motorized and sailing vessels that gently stream along near the shore for the spectator's pleasure. Simply grab a spot along the water from Crissy Field to Pier 39 and watch these lovely boats—some of which are true antiques—float past and announce the start of the season.

Saint Stupid's Day Parade
www.saintstupid.com

This is not your typical, National Beer Company–sponsored parade. The First Church of the Last Laugh, a loose collective of weirdoes and cultural muck-rakers, gathers every April Fool's Day in colorful costumes to toss pennies and socks in front of the Stock Exchange and the Transamerica Building and to otherwise mock the staunch Downtown financial institutions. Don't ask. Just show up and revel in the glory of what happens when street theater meets public statement.

The Sisters of Perpetual Indulgence's Easter Celebration
www.thesisters.org

Gay men in campy nun drag may not be how you celebrated Easter while growing up, but it should become a part of your holiday tradition today. When the weather is cooperative in Dolores Park, kids hunt for colorful eggs, neighbors chill on the lawn, and the annual Hunky Jesus contest winner is crowned—in thorns, of course.

MAY

Carnaval Parade
www.carnavalsf.com

Shimmering bikinis and feathers are the hallmark of this Mission District annual parade, and paired with the incredible music and manageable crowds, this is one you won't want to miss. Brazilian, Caribbean, and Latin American cultures come together to celebrate the pre-Lent holiday—with the common sense to do it this month, instead of in February, where the weather would prohibit the showgirl attire and dampen the desire to shake your rump.

Cinco de Mayo Celebration
www.sfcincodemayo.com/

Sponsored by Mission Neighborhood Centers and packed with vendors and partiers of all colors and creeds, SF's annual Cinco de Mayo festival is a must-go. Afterwards, join the throngs of people hitting the bars until late in the night.

KFOG KaBoom!
www.kfog.com

This local rock 'n' roll radio station features this free outdoor concert and fireworks extravaganza every year to thousands of appreciative "Fogheads." Get there early to stake your spot along the waterfront, as the crowds pack in from all over the Bay Area for the free show.

San Francisco Bay to Breakers
www.ingbaytobreakers.com

This long-standing SF tradition is a race of runners and walkers that traverses the entire width of the city, ending in a huge party and celebration in Golden Gate Park. It costs money to enter the race, but the real treat is watching it, which is gratis citywide. Though the event brings in some real and spirited athletes, the main attraction is the creative costuming, the beer drinking, and those who choose to run the race in the raw.

JUNE

Haight Ashbury Street Fair
www.haightstreetfair.org

The first in the summer series of neighborhood street gatherings, this one has no admission fee but instead features pricey beverages, heaps of vending, and lots of free music and crowd gawking. Note that parking can be a nightmare.

Juneteenth Festival
www.sfjuneteenth.org

This street festival of the Fillmore District is a celebration of the history of African Americans in SF and a preservation of this historic jazz district. Come one, come all for music, food, and special promotions from neighborhood merchants.

North Beach Festival
www.sfnorthbeach.org

Though there's been quite a bit of controversy in recent years about the sales of alcohol during the celebration, this is still one of the more popular neighborhood festivals featuring—you guessed it—free music, vendors galore, a massive crowd, and a showcase of local merchants.

San Francisco Pride Celebration & Parade
www.sfpride.org

Summer in the city just wouldn't be the same without this giant tourist magnet and local holiday. For two days SF is ruled by the power of the rainbow flag, with parties too numerous to mention from the Castro to the Civic Center, and one of the largest annual parades to boot. So much to do, so little time . . .

JULY

Berkeley Kite Festival
www.highlinekites.com/Berkeley_Kite_Festival

The Berkeley Marina explodes with color in the sky at this annual event suitable to entertain the entire family. Sponsored by a kite shop, enthusiasts will be blown away by the aerial display, flying contests, and lessons for beginners new to the string and tail.

Fillmore Street Jazz Festival
www.fillmorejazzfestival.com

A massive street happening with 300 arts and crafts vendors, heaps of live music, and, of course, free jazz in the street.

Fourth of July Waterfront Festival
www.pier39.com

Nothing says summer like fireworks over the water, and that's what draws the crowds here in droves. This gathering has a more family-friendly vibe than most, with loads of free, live entertainment, kids' activities, and lovely views all day and all evening.

AUGUST

Jerry Day
www.jerryday.org

Uh-huh. That Jerry. Garcia. Of the Grateful Dead. The Bay Area simply cannot get enough of this musical legend, so the devoted gather every year in the Excelsior, the place of his birth, for a mecca of sorts, featuring live music (of course), food, and craft vendors of the hippy persuasion.

Nihonmachi Street Fair
www.nihonmachistreetfair.org

Another summer festival in Japantown, this time featuring the foods and culture of several Asian cultures, including Korea and the Philippines.

SEPTEMBER

Folsom Street Fair
www.folsomstreetfair.com

Consider this a celebration of the leather daddy lifestyle and the place to wear your buttless chaps in public. At least it was. This has become a safe-for-tourists hit parade of what used to be the pride festival for SF's leather community, though now the real experts on the subject celebrate at the Up Your Alley street fest on Dore Alley in July. Still, in addition to all of the usual festival fare, you can be flogged publicly for just a few dollars, and you can stock up on fur-lined restraints in a jiffy.

Tour de Fat
www.sfbike.org/fat

The Catch: This is a free event, but donations are requested.

It's a helluva time on two wheels. The San Francisco Bicycle Coalition adds juice to their chain by doing the following: donning crazy costumes suitable for bike riding and drinking beer. Of course, all cyclists are welcome, the beer is sponsored, and there are live music and stage performances of an edgier stripe.

San Francisco Zinefest
www.sfzinefest.com

This event caters to those involved with or interested in small, independent, and underground publishing. Though the focus is mostly zines, this 2-day happening speaks to anyone involved in DIY print media. Activities include perusing exhibits (free) and zine sales (cheap!) and workshops that encourage knowledge-share in this community (reasonable).

OCTOBER

Castro Street Fair
www.castrostreetfair.org

Yes, another street fair, but this one has dance music and a gayer bend.

Fiesta on the Hill
www.fiestaonthehill.com

Family fun at its finest, this street fair of the Bernal Heights community features a well-kept petting zoo, pony rides, a pumpkin patch, and loads of multiculti family fun. It costs nothing to attend, and all performances are free, but partial proceeds benefit the Bernal Heights Neighborhood Center. Note that no alcohol is served or allowed at this event.

Fleet Week
http://fleetweek.us/fleetweek

Thousands of sailors come into town, the Blue Angels make the sky rumble from above, and regardless of how you feel about the military, the sight of aerial acrobatics will take your breath away. Official celebrations happen at the Marina Green and Pier 39, but anyone with ears will have no choice but to participate in this weekend-long event.

Grace Cathedral's Blessing of the Animals
www.gracecathedral.org

The Catch: The service fills up quickly, so get there early if you and Fido actually want to get in.

As is the tradition in the Catholic Church, this month is the celebration of St. Francis, and that means that dogs, cats, rabbits, and even horses step inside this, one of SF's most stunning and enormous houses of worship, to be blessed for another year.

NOVEMBER

Day of the Dead Celebration
Annually on November 2
www.sfcincodemayo.com/

A free, no-alcohol celebration of all those who have passed, this annual Mission neighborhood event is studded with artists, altars, candles, and costumes and lasts late into the night. Enjoyable for the fun-loving and family-oriented alike, this San Francisco tradition is not to be missed.

APPENDIX A:

SAN FRANCISCO RECREATION CENTERS

Always a resource for cheap and low-cost fun and sports, these city-sponsored activity and meeting houses are likely to offer something to cater to your interests. All of these are located in San Francisco.

Alice Chalmers Clubhouse, 670 Brunswick; (415) 337-4711

Argonne Clubhouse, Argonne Playground, 18th Avenue; (415) 666-7008

Balboa Park Community Pool, 51 Havelock Ave.; (415) 337-4701

Bernal Heights Rec Center, 500 Moultrie; (415) 695-5007

Boeddeker Park Clubhouse, 295 Eddy; (415) 292-2019

Bowling Green Clubhouse, Golden Gate Park, Stanyan and Great Highway

Cabrillo Clubhouse, Cabrillo Playground, 38th Avenue; (415) 666-7010

Cayuga Clubhouse, Cayuga Playground, Cayuga and Naglee; (415) 337-4714

Charlie Sava Community Pool, Carl Larsen Park, 19th Avenue and Wawona; (415) 661-6327

Chinese Rec Center, 1199 Mason; (415) 292-2017

Christopher Clubhouse, George Christopher Playground, 5210 Diamond Heights Blvd.; (415) 695-5000

Coffman Community Pool, John McLaren Park, Visitacion and Hahn; (415) 337-9085

Crocker Amazon Clubhouse, Crocker Amazon Playground, Moscow and Italy; (415) 337-4708

Douglass Clubhouse, Douglass Playground, 26th Street and Douglass; (415) 695-5017

Eureka Valley Rec Center, 100 Collingwood; (415) 831-6810

Excelsior Clubhouse, Excelsior Playground, Russia Avenue and Madrid; (415) 337-4709

Fulton Clubhouse, Fulton Playground, 27th Avenue and Fulton; (415) 666-7009

Garfield Square Clubhouse, Garfield Square Community Pool, 26th Street and Harrison; (415) 695-5010

Gere Friend Rec Center SoMa, 270 6th St.; (415) 554-9532

GGP Golf Course Clubhouse, Golden Gate Park, Stanyan and Great Highway; (415) 751-8987

Gilman Clubhouse, Gilman Playground, Gilman Avenue and Griffith; (415) 467-4566

Glen Park Rec Center, Bosworth and O'Shaughnessy; (415) 337-4705

Gleneagles Golf Course Clubhouse, John McLaren Park, Mansell and Visitacion; (415) 587-8987

Golden Gate Park Senior Center, 6101 Fulton near 37th Avenue; (415) 666-7015

Grattan Clubhouse, Grattan Playground, 1180 Stanyan; (415) 753-7039

Hamilton Community Pool, Hamilton Playground, Geary and Steiner; (415) 292-2008

Hamilton Rec Center, Hamilton Playground, 1900 Geary Blvd.

Harvey Milk Recreational Arts Building, Duboce Park, 50 Scott; (415) 554-9523

Hayes Valley Rec Center, Hayes Valley Playground, Hayes and Buchanan; (415) 554-9526

Helen Wills Clubhouse, Helen Wills Playground, Broadway and Larkin Streets; (415) 359-1281

Herz Clubhouse, Herz Playground, 1700 Visitacion and Hahn; (415) 337-4705

J. P. Murphy Clubhouse, J. P. Murphy Playground, 1960 9th Avenue; (415) 753-7099

Jackson Clubhouse, Jackson Playground, 17th Street and Arkansas; (415) 554-9527

James Rolph Jr. Fieldhouse, James Rolph Jr. Playground, Potrero and Cesar Chavez; (415) 695-5018

Joe DiMaggio Clubhouse, Joe DiMaggio Playground, 651 Lombard; (415) 391-0437

John Muir Schoolyard, 380 Webster; (415) 241-6335

Jose Coronado Clubhouse, Jose Coronado Playground, 21st Street and Folsom; (415) 695-5016

Joseph Lee Rec Center, 1395 Mendell St.; (415) 822-9040

Julius Kahn Clubhouse, Julius Kahn Playground, West Pacific Avenue and Spruce; (415) 292-2004

Junipero Serra Clubhouse, Junipero Serra Playground, 300 Stonecrest Dr.; (415) 337-4713

Kezar Pavilion, Golden Gate Park, 755 Stanyan; (415) 753-7032

Laurel Hill Clubhouse, Laurel Hill Playground, Euclid and Collins; (415) 666-7007

Lincoln Park Golf Course Clubhouse, 34th Avenue and Clement; (415) 221-9911

Louis Sutter Clubhouse, Louis Sutter Playground, Wayland and Yale; (415) 584-6106

Margaret S. Hayward Clubhouse, Margaret S. Hayward Playground, 1016 Laguna; (415) 292-2018

Martin Luther King Jr. Pool, Bayview Playground, 3rd Street and Armstrong; (415) 822-2807

McCoppin Square Clubhouse, 24th Avenue and Taraval

Merced Heights Clubhouse, Byxbee and Shields; (415) 337-4718

Midtown Terrace Clubhouse, Clarendon and Olympia Way; (415) 753-7036

Milton Meyers Rec Center, 200 Middle Point Rd.; (415) 285-1415

Minnie and Lovie Ward Rec Center, Ocean View Playground, Capitol and Montana; (415) 337-4710

Miraloma Clubhouse, Omar and Sequoia Way; (415) 337-4704

Mission Community Pool and Clubhouse, 19th Street and Linda; (415) 641-2841

Mission Rec Center, 2450 Harrison; (415) 695-5012, (415) 695-5013

Mission Recreation Center, 745 Treat; (415) 695-5014, (415) 695-5015

Moscone Rec Center, 1800 Chestnut; (415) 292-2045

North Beach Swimming Pool, Joe DiMaggio Playground, 651 Lombard; (415) 391-0407

Palega Rec Center, 500 Felton; (415) 468-2875

Parque Ninos Unidos Clubhouse, 23rd Street and Treat; (415) 282-7461

Pine Lake Park Clubhouse, Sloat Boulevard and Vale; (415) 753-7003

Portsmouth Square Clubhouse, Washington and Kearny; (415) 773-1869

Potrero Hill Rec Center, 801 Arkansas; (415) 695-5009

Presidio Heights Clubhouse, Clay and Walnut; (415) 292-2005

Randall Museum, Corona Heights, Roosevelt and Museum Way; (415) 554-9600

Richmond Playground Clubhouse, 149 18th Ave.; (415) 666-7013

Richmond Rec Center, 251 18th Ave.; (415) 666-7020

Rochambeau Clubhouse, 24th Avenue and Lake; (415) 666-7012

Rossi Community Pool, Angelo J. Rossi Playground, Arguello and Anza; (415) 666-7014

Sandy Tatum Clubhouse, Lake Merced Park, Lake Merced Boulevard; (415) 664-4690

Sharon Arts Studio, Golden Gate Park, Sharon Meadow

Silver Terrace Clubhouse, Thornton and Bayshore; (415) 467-0478

Silver Tree Day Camp, Glen Park, Diamond and Farnum; (415) 337-4717

SoMa Eugene Friend Rec Center, 270 6th St.; (415) 554-9532

South Sunset Clubhouse, 40th Avenue and Vicente; (415) 753-7037

St. Mary's Rec Center, Murray and Justin Drive; (415) 695-5006

Sunnyside Clubhouse, Teresita Avenue and Melrose; (415) 337-4720

Sunset Rec Center, 2201 Lawton; (415) 753-7098

Tenderloin Rec Center, 570 Ellis; (415) 753-2761

Upper Noe Rec Center, Day and Sanchez; (415) 970-8061

Visitacion Valley Clubhouse, Visitacion Valley Playground, 251 Leland; (415) 239-2392

Visitacion Valley Community Center Rec Center, 50 Raymond Ave.; (415) 467-6400

Wawona Clubhouse, 901 Wawona St. at 20th Avenue; (415) 242-5200

West Portal Clubhouse, Ulloa and Lenox; (415) 753-7038

West Sunset Rec Center, 3223 Ortega; (415) 753-7047

Willie Woo Woo Wong Clubhouse, 850 Sacramento; (415) 274-0202

Woh Hei Yuen Rec Center, 922 Jackson; (415) 989-4442

Youngblood Coleman Clubhouse, Mendell and Galvez; (415) 695-5005

APPENDIX B:

BAY AREA COMMUNITY & CULTURAL CENTERS

While not every activity at these gathering places is a free one, many of these houses of neat culture offer some kind of community outreach at low or no cost as a way to spark widespread interest in their own unique style of dance, language, film, food, etc. Check their calendars, get on their mailing lists, and get out there to explore the many multiculti faces that this city has to offer.

African American Art and Culture Complex of San Francisco, 762 Fulton St., Suite 300; (415) 922-2049; www.aaacc.org

Alliance Française of San Francisco, 1345 Bush St.; (415) 775-7755; www.afsf.com

Arab Cultural and Community Center, 2 Plaza St.; (415) 664-2200; www.arabculturalcenter.org

Asian Pacific Islander Cultural Center, 934 Brannan St.; (415) 864-4120; www.apiculturalcenter.org

Bayview Opera House Ruth Williams Memorial Theatre, 4705 3rd St.; (415) 824-0386; www.bayviewoperahouse.org

CELLspace, 2050 Bryant St.; (415) 742-6416; www.cellspace.org

Chinese Culture Center of San Francisco, 750 Kearny St., 3rd floor; (415) 986-1822; www.c-c-c.org

Croatian American Cultural Center, 60 Onondaga Ave.; (510) 649-0941; www.slavonicweb.org

Goethe-Institut San Francisco, 530 Bush St., 2nd floor; (415) 263-8760; www.goethe.de/sanfrancisco

Hang Ah Hillside Cultural Center, 883 Sacramento St.; www.hangah-hillside.net

Israel Center, 121 Steuart St.; (415) 512-6203; www.israelcentersf.org

Italian Cultural Institute of San Francisco, 814 Montgomery St.; (415) 788-7142; www.iicsanfrancisco.esteri.it/IIC_Sanfrancisco

Japanese Cultural and Community Center of Northern California, 1840 Sutter St., Suite 201; (415) 567-5505; www.jcccnc.org

Jewish Community Center of San Francisco, 3200 California St.; (415) 292-1200; www.jccsf.org

Korean Youth Cultural Center, 4216 Telegraph Ave., Oakland; (510) 652-4964; www.kycc.net

La Peña Cultural Center, 3105 Shattuck Ave., Berkeley; (510) 849-2568; www.lapena.org

Mission Cultural Center for Latino Arts, 2868 Mission St.; (415) 821-1155; www.missionculturalcenter.org

Native American Cultural Center, P.O. Box 14408, San Francisco CA 94114; www.nativecc.com

The Norwegian Club, 1900 Fell St.; (415) 668-8608, (415) 668-1558; www .norwegianclub.org

Pacific Islanders' Cultural Center, 1016 Lincoln Blvd., #5; (415) 281-0221 (voice messages only); www.pica-org.org (They encourage correspondence via e-mail at info@pica-org.org.)

Queer Cultural Center, 934 Brannan St.; (415) 864-4124; www.queercultural center.org

Russian Center of San Francisco, 2450 Sutter St.; (415) 921-7631; www .russiancentersf.com

SomArts Cultural Center, 934 Brannan St.; (415) 863-1414; www.somarts .org

United Irish Cultural Center, 2700 45th Ave.; (415) 661-2700; www.irish centersf.org

APPENDIX C:

ADDITIONAL RESOURCES
FOR EVERY CHEAP BASTARD

96Hours
www.sfgate.com/96hours

Thursday print supplement to the *San Francisco Chronicle;* many free events.

The City Dish
www.sfcitydish.com

Tune in to great specials, 2-for-1s, coupons, and downright giveaways in food and drink.

Craigslist.org
For everything—events, goods, services, classes, etc.

FunCheapSF
http://sf.funcheap.com

Subscribe (for free, of course) to this weekly listserv to find out what free happenings and opportunities await for your social calendar this week. An indispensable resource for any tightwad. Events, food, etc.

San Francisco Bay Guardian
www.sfbg.com

In print every Wednesday; some free events.

San Francisco Weekly
www.sfweekly.com

In print every Wednesday; some free events.

SF's My Open Bar
http://sf.myopenbar.com

This delivers what it promises for boozehounds who seek someone else to pick up the tab. Events, food.

SFStation.com
Some free events.

Squidlist
www.squidlist.org

Many free events.

INDEX